The
Province
of Sociology
Freedom and Constraint

Bernard Rosenberg

Willett Professor of Liberal Education,
University of Chicago

The Province of Sociology
Freedom and Constraint

THOMAS Y. CROWELL COMPANY · NEW YORK
ESTABLISHED 1834

One for the girls: Sarah,
Leona, Judith, Deena, Rebecca,
and in memory of Regina and
Rachel

S‌ociologists, as Bernard Rosenberg brilliantly demonstrates in this book, do not agree and never have agreed on a definition of sociology. For such a definition implies a program for work to be done (and the methods, materials, and ideas to be employed), a relationship to other disciplines, and, perhaps, more basically, an attitude toward society—toward its preservation, reformation, or reconstruction. About all of this there has never been any uniformity.

While sociology as a discipline is less than a hundred years old, the issues that divide it, except in its more technical phases, go back at least to classical Greece and the Old Testament. These issues, the perennial problems of man, weave their way through Western philosophy, especially through the philosophy of natural law and the Enlightenment, and remain the central bone of contention not only in contemporary sociology, but among all those immersed in the cultural and social revolution of our time.

Auguste Comte, the first man to use the term sociology, felt that by the comparative study of societies, one could discover the natural laws governing society and by so doing, predict and control the

Foreword

operation of society, that is, make it amenable to reason. Karl Marx, also a precursor of sociology, felt he had discovered the historical laws that governed capitalism. On the basis of this knowledge he could, by organizing a disciplined political party and making a revolution, help create the conditions under which society would at last be subject to control.

The social philosophers, intellectuals, and clergymen who were the forerunners of sociology were ideologists, revolutionaries, conservatives, or reformers, with explicit values, biases, premises, and programs. Sociology, as it evolved into a separate discipline, developed an ideology of reason and of science, and attempted to justify itself quite self-consciously by articulating methods, concepts, and principles designed to free sociology from the ideological commitments and biases of its precursors. Yet a major aspect of twentieth-century sociology focused on the scientific solutions of social problems by methods short of revolution; such solutions were most often based upon a liberal reform of the structure of society. Applied sociologists attempted to provide scientific solutions to the technical problems of many people, but mostly those who would pay the bill for supporting sociologists and their research. Such sociology was necessarily conservative, and nowhere was it more conservative than in the Soviet Union, which only adopted "scientific sociology" without reservation after its original revolutionary sociology had paved the way for a new regime whose victory made communism into an established conservative social order.

In the United States, between the 1940s and the mid-1960s, the dominant ideas in sociology stemmed from the nature of social order and its overall coordination and integration. Reflecting age-old concerns in social philosophy, social theorists like Talcott Parsons attempted, by the use of presumably scientific concepts, to answer such questions as: How is society possible? How does it function? How does it maintain itself without flying apart? What are the conditions for successful coordination of societies? The answers provided were in the form of abstract, general models (or blueprints or maps) of a hypothetical functioning society called the social system. Such models, once developed, could then be applied to the description and analysis of historical societies in order to explain or improve them.

These models derived from the notion that society was based upon a fundamental consensus or agreement about values, which allowed individuals and groups voluntaristically pursuing their own ends to modify their goals and actions because of their acceptance of a common culture and their agreement on ultimate values such that major conflicts and splits in society were avoided. Each major element (or structural unit) in the social system tended to support other elements, and the system as a whole developed "system maintaining functions," special mechanisms that enabled the system to operate in an orderly, continuous way. To the extent that conflict occurred, it was deviant, exceptional, or secondary, the product of "structural strains" and the bases for new forms of societal integration.

Structural functionalism and functionalism, as these theories are called, were not without opponents. Some social theorists emphasized that conflict was not merely a deviant element in the development of society, but was central to the operation and evolution of society. Other opponents emphasized that force and repression were dominant means of social control, and value consensus and agreement were of secondary importance, the product of "brainwashing" and propaganda, which the voluntarist euphemistically called socialization. Still other critics emphasized that structural functionalism was unrealistic because it presented an essentially static model of a society that maintains itself in a self-sustaining equilibrium, whose operation results in the reinforcement of its central system, with change occurring only by slow and gradual accretion. Another criticism turned on the notion that society or the social system appeared to have an abstract intelligence that seemed to be located somewhere in the system, but not in the population dwelling within the system. Thus, the idea that a "system" maintains or reinforces itself or rewards its members or has goals of its own suggests a central agency or intelligence that at best can only be located in a specific organization and not in the "system" itself. But such an organization or agency is never specified in structural-functionalist thought.

Finally, functionalism was criticized because its models were so abstract and general that they did not apply to any particular historical society but only to the abstract models themselves. According to this criticism, one would have to abandon functionalism just as soon as one tried to describe in detail the specific operation of any particular society, simply because societies do not exist at the abstract level of the models used by functionalists. Many of the critics argued, in addition, that on a political level, functionalism emphasized (and thus justified) the functional necessity of the established order, with its dominant classes and leadership groups, and it thereby devalued dissidents and deviants. It appeared to value established norms, culture, ideas, and ideologies, often for no other reason than that they are the basis of any societal consensus. In emphasizing order, consensus, and integration, it devalued change, innovation, disagreement, and revolutionary or radical activity. Additionally, its emphasis on consensus could be viewed as an emphasis on conformity to any system or order that was already established.

Yet, it was not these arguments and polemics that were decisive in the decline of functionalism. Rather, it was the previously submerged conflict, a "cultural revolution," violence and dissension that surfaced in the 1960s, that made much of the sociology of that era irrelevant. A theory based on value agreement or consensus seemed to be grotesque in an age of "revolution," assassination, violence, strikes, riots, and the repression that may have caused, attended, and ensued from the violence of that decade. For a social theory to be relevant, it must "make sense of," be related to, and explain the salient facts that seem so obvious even to a casually interested observer of the times. Functionalism was palpably out of touch with a society dominated by violence and dissension.

Whether we like it or not, structural functionalism and functionalist theories are moribund. And sociologists, among others, are faced with the task of reconstructing social theory in a way that makes it descriptive of the realities it purportedly reflects.

The decline of functionalism did not automatically generate theories that would replace it. Many of the new theories designed to replace functionalism were part and parcel of the "revolution" of the sixties. Some were mindless calls to action, programs for a new sociology that would create the revolution called for, but they did little to explain or describe the society out of which that revolution would emerge. They substituted name calling and the repetition of nineteenth-century clichés for thought, description, or analysis. Others are prescriptive, that is, their authors are preoccupied with constructing models of an ideal society that will exist the day after their hoped-for political or cultural revolution is realized; and since these ideologies are prescriptive, they need not concern facts, description, or reality. Moreover, some do not concern even the means by which a new society is to be attained. A voluntarism more rarefied than that imagined by functionalists allows dreamers to "think away" these realities. "If only we opt out of the system, do our own thing, we can, by changing ourselves, change the whole system, because we are the system." Yet if this argument were valid, it would be true for the past as well as for the future. And the failure of individual consciousnesses in the past to create ideal social systems exists as a problem for all those who would hope to do so in the future. Certainly functionalists argued that consciousnesses, i.e., value agreements, determined society; and the criticism leveled against functionalism must apply as well to the new utopianism of prescriptive sociology.

Those who argue for a new society by advocating or defending revolutionary violence need to face their own argument that structural functionalism is wrong because that theory ignores the violence, repression, and conflict on which contemporary society is based; for they argue in favor of the same methods they abhor in the established society that they would overthrow. They argue, like all idealistic militants, that this war (against capitalist society) is the war to end war; that this revolution is one to make further revolution and repression unnecessary. They refuse to recognize that much of the repression, violence, and oppression in the past has been based upon ideologies of liberation, and that almost all idealistic revolutionaries have become either the victims of their own methods, tactics, and strategies or the new oppressors. Moreover, as the techniques of revolution and reaction have been perfected by means of the study of past revolutionary successes and failures, the amount of violence and repression produced by successful revolutions appears to increase. Modern totalitarianism is far more efficient than the totalitarianisms of the past, and nearly all modern totalitarians began as idealistic revolutionaries.

Thus radical sociology emphasizes the repressiveness of the past and the liberation of the future; the conflict and divisiveness of the present and the organic unity and freedom from alienation to be achieved in the future. It emphasizes the static characteristics of received social theory and societies of the past, and the necessity and desirability for change right now and in toto to achieve the ideal society. All too often change also becomes an abstract ideal, without any clear definition of the specific changes desired. Radical sociology frequently condemns the violence of existing societies but glorifies violence controlled by radicals as a means of creating new but usually unspecified social and political institutions. It attacks the narrow rationality, the narrow intellectualism of modern industrial society, a society that is viewed as denying the emotional, sensual, poetic, and myth-making faculties of man—while "planning" for or demanding a new society that will be reasonable and rational.

If structural functionalism was conservative, if it overemphasized consensus, social statics, and social order, radical sociology makes the opposite (yet the same) errors; for in taking its point of departure from structural functionalism, it shifts the focus of the very same analysis from past to future tense and vice versa. It values consensus as much as do structural functionalists but locates that consensus in the future; it values a higher rationality and in a vague stasis that will be achieved in the indefinite future, but one that also allows the very permissiveness that is viewed as repressive in the present.

Bernard Rosenberg, in this volume, addresses himself to the same problems that engage both the waning functionalists and the radical sociologists of our age. But his approach differs from theirs. They see society as a phenomenon based upon polarities: order-disorder, statics-change, freedom-oppression, conformity-spontaneity, unity-diversity, etc.; and each makes in his selection of central concepts virtually an all-or-nothing choice of one extreme in each set of polarities. Professor Rosenberg's central approach is that in historical societies such all-or-nothing choices do not exist: each extreme contains its own opposite.

Thus no society is possible without some minimal form of consensus, and no society exists without some external form of social control. All societies are therefore in some way repressive, but all repression breeds the desire for freedom. All societies induce some conformity, but the same repression that is necessary to produce conformity produces spontaneity, innovation, and the desire for self-realization. No society can by its very nature be static, and the very operation of society produces changes; but all social change is conditioned by the past out of which change occurs. While society is based, to some extent, on the operation of law, the very operation of society produces the violation of law; and the pillars of society as well as the defenders of law and order are among the violators of the law.

The existence of society is dependent on belief in myth, fictions, and appearances—"living lies"; yet conflict between "appearance and reality" is a major social reality. Disbelief results in the creation of new "beliefs" that coexist with old "lies," and both hold together and yet tear apart the society, which generates further social change.

But there is more than the fact that each extreme in a given set of polarities contains its own opposite that is significant. More importantly, all of the various *sets* of polarities affect each other. Any pattern of social change is likely to affect the nature and degree of consensus or repression in society, the amount and kind of deviancy, conformity, crime, and delinquency, etc.; and each of these developments can be considered a social change. Hence, society is interlocking and interlacing, but what interlace and interlock are continuous patterns of change, conflict and consensus, conformity and spontaneity, repression and freedom, crime, deviancy, law and order, and their many correlatives.

The implications of this mode of analysis are manifold. In the first place, it provides the grounds for some degree of optimism, though that optimism may be tempered: for no society can, in the long run, be totally repressive. The "normal" operation of society produces the strains, the contradictions, the inefficiencies that make freedom possible; and even repressiveness, social control, and "brainwashing" produce both the countervalues and inevitable reactions that make for spontaneity, innovation, and creativity. But limitations in optimism are also inherent in Professor Rosenberg's position. In the first instance the very social machinery that liberates men and makes progress possible also contains within it the possibility of new and different forms of social and psychological repression. Even affluence, which in many ways liberates men from poverty, ignorance, and disease, makes them susceptible to subtle forms of personality absorption, conformity, and to a withering away of the will to use their potentialities to create or engage in socially or personally useful activities.

A further ground for pessimism in Professor Rosenberg's position can be found in its implications for absolute personal and social liberation; for his analysis suggests that such freedom from the past is impossible. Regardless of intentions, high-mindedness, or sincerity, the believer in absolute social change brings with him attitudes and values that could only have been acquired in the past. And, as we have already suggested, the means and methods, the strategy and tactics used to create social change become the bases for a social order that emerges from the use of these tactics and strategies. Therefore, the believers in absolute freedom become the creators of social orders that are likely, for a time, to be monstrously repressive. But even here the process of change operates against a monolithic society. The areas of freedom that do emerge frequently emerge against the will of its liberators.

Yet, if absolute oppression and absolute freedom are not possible in a living social system, this does not mean that social action, reform, and attempts at amelioration are not desirable or possible. On the contrary, since we know that society presents itself to us in the form of detailed, specific customs, organizations, policies, privileges, rights, duties, injustices, defects, delinquencies, and deficiencies, we are obligated to address ourselves to very specific conditions which we would like to correct. Reform, social action, and the correction of deficiencies in society need to be as specific, informed, intelligent, organized, and disciplined as the conditions and groups against which we protest. This is all the more necessary if we know that absolute idealism, by nature unintelligent and uninformed, regardless of its proponents' sincerity, is likely to yield evils of a magnitude equal to or greater than those that already exist.

Joseph Bensman
The City College of the City University of New York

Contents

Conflicting Conceptions of Sociology

WHAT *is* sociology? If laymen or beginners feel uncertain and confused about how to answer that question, let them be at ease. When asked to define his subject matter, the thoughtful student of sociology suddenly finds himself tongue-tied—or garrulous, pedantic, and obscure. After approximately a century of gestation, birth, growth, and development, the field remains diffuse and problematic. Even today any attempt to establish clear sociological boundaries must be considered premature. Whosoever claims definitiveness for sociology succeeds only in revealing his own naïveté. Nor will an operational definition serve the purpose. For, although sociology is surely what sociologists do, they are more than ever at odds about the propriety if not the validity and legitimacy of their professional preoccupations.

Disarray, to put it gently, is the condition that prevails in an amorphous discipline whose very premises, postulates, methods, and findings are in constant dispute. Fact-fetishists, humanists, functionalists, and structuralists, behaviorists, symbolic interactionists, positivists, and phenomenologists strenuously seek an intellectual ascend-

1
What Is Sociology?

ancy none has been able to gain. Ethically neutral observers scorn politically committed activists who reciprocate in kind. Macrosociologists with an illimitable range and microsociologists burrowing into tiny corners vie for academic hegemony. Those who make much of flux, change, friction, and evolution have little in common with their antagonists who emphasize order, stability, equilibrium, and consensus.

The sociologist is likely to rationalize, dogmatize, and polemicize while vigorously defending his own position in the midst of a chaotic diversity. Given this background, or this battleground, it is most becoming of him to combine Socratic modesty with free-floating skepticism. We know terribly little, and that little looks more doubtful the better we know it. Meanwhile, as proponents of revolution and champions of the status quo embrace our teachings with about equal fervor, more and more of us insiders put sociology itself on trial. Indiscriminate acceptance within the academy *and* within the revolutionary cadre, by learned and previously hostile colleagues *and* by a half-educated public, mounts so steadily that one's own cries of caution go unheeded. I shall argue that sociology has something intrinsically valuable to offer in the here-and-now. To exaggerate that claim, however, is to produce vast embarrassment among men who feel unworthy of the approval lavished upon them. Therefore it should be said without equivocation that sociology cannot begin to control, let alone make, unmake, or remake the vale of tears and laughter that mankind inhabits. Ideologues of every coloration—left, center, and right—businessmen, managers, rebels, functionaries, public and private officials, subversives, supporters, and detractors: Beware. The sociologist you flatter and pet, reward and pamper may be pleased, but only if he shares your inflated expectations about the goods his firm is not now (and never will be) capable of delivering.

The Classical Outlook

Recently a British sociologist remarked that our enterprise, with its multitude of "Founding Fathers," has succeeded only in begetting stillborn children. An equally bitter but more familiar epigram originated some years ago on this side of the Atlantic, according to which sociology is a field with many approaches and few arrivals. While such harsh judgments are somewhat excessive, the kernel of truth in them is undeniable. Not long after its inception in the nineteenth and early twentieth centuries, sociology enjoyed a Golden Age—by whose inspired bearers it is still sustained. As titans like Max Weber, Émile Durkheim, Herbert Spencer, Karl Marx, and Georg Simmel recede in time, their legacy of ideas looms larger than ever. Contemporary sociology battens on them. They are the inexhaustible seedbed out of which theories, hypotheses, concepts, and research designs continue to spring. Furthermore, the "many approaches" engendered by an array of geniuses finally boil down to a single comprehensive approach. Indeed, sociology is important in direct proportion to its successful embodiment of this approach. It will be our central concern in all that follows.

The first and second generation of French, German, English, Italian, and American sociologists were pioneers staking out new scholarly territory. Biologists, economists, historians, theologians, engineers, philosophers, psychologists, autodidacts, and academicians independently arose to proclaim the advent of what they regarded as a new science. Each and severally, one specialist after another turned himself into a sociological generalist. Hitherto neglected or unknown areas were henceforth to be explored on a rigorous and systematic basis. Hopes ran high that a Copernican, if not a Newtonian or Darwinian turn might soon be taken in the study of human affairs. The version of science then most widely accepted that was applied to "the starry heavens above," and then to all inorganic and organic terrestrial matter, could at last be used to spread "the categorical imperative within." No one tried at first to disentangle descriptive from prescriptive elements—a thorny problem that haunts us to this day. The early formulations contained a quantity of nonsense (that has yet to be wholly eliminated). They also offered a vision, a point of view, a common perspective or a general orientation from which considerable light could be shed on otherwise virtually unintelligible matters. Despite its variegated sources and incompatible components, sociology as such provided *the social or cultural or collective dimension* that so many men of learning had come to feel they needed. The ironic result is that, although sociologists have had great difficulty agreeing among themselves, and may even too often have cross-sterilized one another, their "classical" outlook enriched much else that it touched.

The Rejection of History as the Work of Heroes and Gods

Simmel pointed out that traditional history was no more than a chronicle of great men and gods. Gods did not survive. No serious historian, with the possible exception of Arnold J. Toynbee, would dare any more to affirm Georg Hegel's pious belief in a providential order. *Ist der Weltgeschichte das Weltgerichte?* (History always works out for the best.) To express such a belief is to presuppose the existence of a divine will which, with total benevolence, directs human affairs to an eschatologically ineffable destiny. What historian of our times would not be laughed out of court for coming to his craft with such other-worldly equipment? If he has a taste for theology, his supernaturalism had better be clothed in Manichaean or Gnostic metaphors. That the devil subdued Jehovah and fixed his designs on a godforsaken universe is the kind of fable contemporary readers might find more acceptable. Apart from such quaint fancies and conceits, the Judeo-Christian tradition has little bearing on how history is written in this day and age. Moreover, teleology has gone the way of theology. The historical process as currently expounded leaves no room for a mysterious and undiscoverable purpose. History is just one damn thing after another. It has been disenchanted.

If Hegel, the true believer, is irrelevant to a modern historian, so is Thomas Carlyle, the hero-worshiper. Time, place, and milieu look more significant than great men who, while they sometimes make events, are more thoroughly made by them. In our assessment of the past, great men continue to count, but for much less than they once did. With their shrinkage, history has ceased to be primarily a sequence of military engagements, a succession of monarchs, an account of royal decisions and formal decrees.

Thanks in large measure to the impact of sociology, the focus of history is now noticeably more mundane. As heroes dwindle, family structure, kinship, tribal organization, religious observance, community action, and social stratification come strongly to the fore. The historian attends to lowly and intermediate, not just lordly concerns. In his annals the everyday life of ordinary men and women enjoys greater and greater prominence. This trend has proceeded so far that it is hardly possible anymore to write political, military, intellectual, economic, or art history without also writing social history.

The Emphasis on Social Institutions

The sociological stamp placed on history and historiography may be found in contiguous spheres. A similar broadening of horizons is most pronounced in psychology, economics, political science, and the matrix out of which they all arose—philosophy itself. Individual psychology becomes a contradiction in terms as it shades off into group psychology, and no one can clearly tell where that inquiry stops and sociology begins. Homo economicus, a strange individualist abstracted from qualities erroneously assumed to be inherent in human nature, cannot stand alone. The model from which Adam Smith and his devotees constructed their economic man, that avaricious monster who unintentionally fulfills a divine function, has collapsed. Wherever "anomalies" like panic, depression, nationalism, and war intrude themselves, there the economist must reckon with large social forces. In that sense, all economics is institutional economics.

Sociology and Political Science

So too with politics. Aristotle thought man was preeminently a political animal. Certain classical scholars prefer to translate Aristotle's adjective as "social" rather than "political." When a Greek word is correctly rendered in either of two ways, lexicographers have reason to be distressed. The ambiguity, however, can only please sociologists who reject an unnatural division between politics and society. One dominates the other at any particular time. Under various circumstances, a society is wholly, moderately, or lightly politicized; but always and everywhere politics and society are indivisible.

The staples of political science have long been those of government, its machinery, hierarchy, constitution, and legislation. How laws are decreed, enacted, perpetuated, amended, or abolished; which officeholders are invested with what authority; who coerces whom: none of these questions is obsolete. They bear directly on the field of internal or domestic affairs. Similarly, in international relations, account must be taken of treaties, alliances, diplomatic exchanges, the adjudication of disputes, and much else that takes place on a government-to-government level.

Careful study of such substantive topics can teach us a great deal. And yet we are capable of learning more with the addition of a synthetic overview, which spotlights sociological variables. Our attention is then drawn to the governed as well as the governors. To be sure, political sociology has lately become more fashionable than political economy in part because of a renewed interest in elites and oligarchies. Early in this century, the upper reaches of political power fascinated three brilliant converts to sociology whose *aperçus* continue to suggest hypotheses and stimulate research. The famous trio consisted of Gaetano Mosca, Robert Michels, and Vilfredo Pareto, three conservative intellectuals once dubbed "The Machiavellians." They independently established a lasting sociological concern with the problem of political leadership. That problem, on further examination, could not be extricated from the problem of political followership, to which it was after all indissolubly linked.

Looking down and around at those who were supposed to obey their "betters," whether or not they did so, put sociology onto another track. There it was scarcely possible not to explore the grass-roots of politics. On that terrain, the social undergrowth materialized in all its abundance. We shall presently examine the implications of this discovery.

Sociology and Philosophy

Prima facie, philosophy has contributed far more to sociology than sociology can ever contribute to philosophy. When Alfred North Whitehead said that all philosophy was a footnote to Plato, he spoke in the broadest sense for every legitimate—and every misbegotten—child of philosophy. If to philosophize is to seek wisdom, then that activity will never cease to have its great and crucial place. From metaphysics through epistemology to logic, every branch of philosophy is germane to whatever world view we happen to adopt. Of late, the philosopher has devoted himself above all to his traditional and interminable task, which is that of explication or clarification. How do men arrive at what they consider the truth? Is there an acceptable definition of reality? What exactly does the modern scientist do? Linguistic analysis and symbolic logic are two advanced philosophical techniques for the examination of these issues. While seeming to be far removed from the daily concerns of sentient beings, they bear heavily on all of them. Connections of this order, while noteworthy and demonstrable, are, however, beyond our scope. It is perhaps enough to say that sociologists who do not draw on the capital that philosophy offers seriously risk intellectual bankruptcy.

Not that philosophers from their pre-Socratic beginnings to the present speak in a single, or even a harmonious choral voice. They have no uniform heritage to confer upon us. That to absorb as much philosophy as possible is advisable cannot be gainsaid. For that matter, it is advisable to absorb as much physics or poetry or paleontology or jazz music or criminal argot or—but the list is infinite. The more facets of our universe we grasp and the greater depth with which we grasp them only serve to make us better sociologists. Of philosophy, which may be narrow and esoteric or inclusive and exoteric, one must ask: What philosophy? Whose philosophy?

The English scholar, H. A. Hodges, remarks: "Philosophers have devoted endless trouble to discussing how we come to be aware of physical objects and how far subjective elements enter into our experience of them. They have talked as if our world consisted entirely of such objects, and as if the knowledge of them were our chief intellectual concern. Yet the most significant of our experiences lie in our relations with other people, and the nature and extent of the knowledge which we can have of other people is a question of equal importance with the first." [1] In traditional philosophy, primary and secondary qualities were minutely differentiated, percepts carefully distinguished from concepts, and reality located either in the nervous system or in the external world. This was the stuff of epistemology, and it constituted much, if not most of speculative philosophy. Idealism and realism, as old as Plato and Aristotle, persisted under a multiplicity of labels, obfuscations, permutations, and combinations. Subdued and debased, they are far less with us since the triumph of natural science. Our awareness of physical objects and how we perceive them has long ceased to be prime material for logic-chopping philosophers who have given way to men of science. En route, the likes of David Hume and John Locke, of Immanuel Kant and Johann Fichte and Georg Hegel, of Gottfried von Leibnitz, Baruch Spinoza, and René Descartes are major transitional figures. They do not denigrate the traditional stress on physicality but tend rather to supplement it with an additional stress on personality. They psychologize. The Cartesian "I" in one form or another is their point of departure. Finally, with philosophers like Wilhelm Dilthey, Karl Jaspers, John Dewey, and George Herbert Mead, the sociological "we" and "they" come into their own. By its insistence that consciousness of self and consciousness of others are inseparable, sociology makes a modest down payment on its debt to philosophy. From this point onward no serious discussion of man can proceed very far if it ignores interpersonal, that is to say, social relationships. And they are the special province of sociology.

[1] H. A. Hodges, *The Philosophy of Wilhelm Dilthey* (London: Routledge and Kegan Paul, 1952), p. 34.

vo positivism

Indeed, all the human studies that converge in and make up sociology are a product of this epistemological revolution. If man is more than a biochemical creature or a psychophysical receptor, if he is not merely a collocation of atomic and subatomic particles, then what? Then and only then are we able to see him in all his uniqueness, his quite remarkable particularity and peculiarity. Without our postulating an irreducible difference between man and non-man, there is no justification for sociology or any of its kindred sciences. We must specify and elaborate the nature of this difference, which now more than ever—while dehumanization lurks all about us—commands our interest.

Sociology as "Science"

As social science belatedly appeared in the wake of physical science, so social scientism followed physical scientism. Science changes into scientism when it becomes a god whose devotees replace their ancestral faith with a new secular religion. When scientists or their uncritical admirers no longer regard their laboriously constructed tools as means to a proximate end, they have been overcome by scientism. Plain, profane methodology is so sanctified that it emerges, in Floyd W. Matson's apposite term, as "methodolatry." [2] To make ends of means is serious enough; to worship those means is worse; but the truly hopeless error is to select inadequate or inappropriate means for deification. Auguste Comte who called his brainchild sociology also baptized it as "social physics." In fact, "positivism," another of his neologisms, refers to the direct application to the social sciences of methods perfected in celestial mechanics and other physical or biological sciences. They are perfectly applicable—but only insofar as man is a machine or an animal like all other animals. Beyond that point, they are inapplicable, grotesque, and useless. In physics and chemistry, as in biology and its offshoots (though less so), mathematics is indispensable. Quantitative data, bolstered by mathematical or statistical inferences, are also useful to the sociolo-

[2] Matson is a critical contemporary social scientist.

vs correlation

gist. If he proceeds with due caution, having shown himself to be a virtuoso of quantitative technique, his formulas, tables, graphs, and charts are likely to be harmless. On the other hand, ill-conceived statisticism (which is scientism or positivism-cum-methodologism run wild) can be dangerous. A statistical correlation in and of itself is meaningless. None of us can satisfactorily define intelligence, race, or crime. These are three of the fuzziest nouns in English or any other language, and yet they have been endlessly correlated—almost always to the further detriment of an already oppressed minority group. Thus, to quantify nebulosities is sometimes a harmful pastime. More often, mathematico-statistical methodology is consecrated to the trivia that its practitioners can manipulate. What they do may be dismissed as just a waste of time unless the trivia are confounded with matters of great weight and importance. That they are so confounded with disconcerting frequency exposes every positivistic culprit to book reviewer Clive Entwhistle's barb:

> The sociologist likes to think of himself as a "scientist" in the sense that a physicist or a chemist is a scientist. Indeed, in his anxiety to assume this authoritative role, he has proved himself most willing to jettison every unquantifiable element in the field of human studies. He does not throw out the baby *with* the bath water—he throws out the baby and keeps the bath water for hard chromatographic analysis. The baby is held to be described by the results.[3]

Sociology as a "Humanistic Study"

"Human studies" can help to preserve that baby, leaving the bath water for some more suitable purpose. Entwhistle's caricature hits its mark, but his target has begun to dissolve. The type of sociologist he satirizes appeared mainly between the two World Wars and for awhile thereafter; but even then and even in America, this type failed to enjoy an uncontested monopoly. Lately the pendulum has swung away from those overconfident scholars who thought and taught that facts were nothing but figures, and consequently, that the proper study of mankind was statistics. They have yielded more

[3] *New York Times Book Review* (December 31, 1967).

and more to the kind of sociologist, who while wishing to remain an empiricist, but not a *radical* empiricist, and a realist, but not a *naïve* realist, also thinks of himself as a humanist. And yet only a few years ago, Dennis Wrong and Peter Berger sounded iconoclastic when they proclaimed their devotion to a "humanistic sociology." What should have been a redundant phrase became the battle cry of something subterranean that Wrong literally referred to as an underground. Its numbers have swollen, and they are by now very much aboveground.

On this slippery semantic terrain, the Germans have less of a problem than we do. Besides the broader *Kulturgeschichte, Geistes-wissenschaften* (translatable as the human studies) has long been an acceptable synonym for sociology. The French tradition, despite Comte's conceptual eccentricities, has also been less linguistically troublesome than our own. In France, from the beginning, sociology was *une science morale*. An odd academic compartment? A contradiction in terms? Not at all. *Science morale*, taken to heart, rehumanizes much that the crude positivists strove to dehumanize. It points us once again in the direction that leads to a real *raison d'être* for sociology.

Morale, from the Latin *mos, moris*, and a variety of related derivatives, suggests something special about man that underlies and justifies any study of his conduct. As Crane Brinton, an historian, has put it in a popular treatise on the subject:

> If "conduct" is used consistently to indicate what men do, and "ethics" to indicate their appraisal of the value of their actions, then "moral" may be used to sum up the whole human situation involved in the existence of both conduct and evaluation of conduct, of both the "is" and the "ought" in human awareness of past, present and future.[4]

And with that we are thrust by Professor Brinton into the specifically sociological universe of discourse. For, as he says, "Our moral awareness is a state of tension familiar to us all, no matter what our religion or our philosophy. . . ." Moreover, "Morality is at once a part of man's being and the whole of it."

[4] Crane Brinton, *A History of Morals* (New York: Harcourt, Brace & World, 1959), p. 25.

> As moral beings, we all bear an uneasy burden from which most of us can hardly escape with serenity. . . . In particular, we cannot avoid thinking about morals, yet we cannot, peace to Spinoza, think about them, demonstrate them, after the manner of mathematics.[5]

Can we think about and demonstrate them after the manner of social science? One hopes so. For, if not, to paraphrase George Bernard Shaw, the sociologist would be better off using his breath to cool his soup. In sociological jargon, morals and other rules of conduct have come to be known as "norms." The analysis of norms makes up a sizable part of our enterprise. Such analysis presupposes that human conduct, whether conformist or not, is substantially normative. When men are compliant or defiant, imitative or innovative, cooperative or competitive (and so on through the whole gamut of possibilities), they respond to rules that other men have made. The rules, or norms, are simply there. But they are there to accept or to reject, to balance, to juggle, or to circumvent and evade. In the swirling flux of social life all of us mechanically abide by some norms while more or less deliberately flouting others. To obey is to give to our acts that irreducible measure of predictability without which human beings could not interact. Not to obey, in whole or in part, is to inject a variable element of unpredictability, contingency, and uncertainty into our affairs. The universal consequence of this mixture is a condition in which order and creativity, necessity and freedom are omnipresent. Together they suffuse the social action of human beings which, whether rule-regulated or rule-violative, is almost always normative. From narrow conformity to radical nonconformity, our lives are saturated with rules.

But for a certain, and until recently, modish, overemphasis on the means by which conformity alone is exacted, we would be ill-advised to dwell upon this sociological commonplace. Accounting for conformity, in no matter how limited a way, is no small accomplishment. Those sociologists who continue to struggle with the complications of that process deserve our respect. We gladly extend it even while chiding them for their one-sidedness. Many are heirs of Durkheim who simplify the cultural determinism which that master incon-

---

[5] Loc. cit.

sistently expounded. As usual, these epigone convert complex ideas into tidy doctrines while overlooking a welter of difficulties the original thinker knew he could not avoid.

Durkheim and "Social Facts"

Émile Durkheim dealt with "social facts" that he took to be binding rules or norms that are prior and exterior to us as individuals. He maintained that these facts, projected as legal codes, folk sayings, oral or written prescriptions and prohibitions were really things, or at least should be treated as if they were. These things comprise the social situation into which we are born. Their great weight is irresistible. It causes each one of us to be reborn as Homo sociologicus, a repository of moral principles, a walking dictionary of popular aphorisms, proverbs, articles of faith, and communal standards of taste; a personification of religious, metaphysical, and political beliefs, customs, conventions, and traditions. This repertoire of "things," along with what we would nowadays call our material culture, i.e., technology, is the social heritage. Every newborn infant, from the moment that bundle of protoplasm emits its first cry, is subject to relentless social pressure. From first to last, but most effectively during the period of greatest plasticity, it will be constrained and coerced, tamed and civilized. No wonder "culture," the modern label for Durkheim's "society," has sometimes been defined as castration. It has also been claimed, with reason from this angle, that human beings are like horses that need to be spayed before they can be domesticated.

Social control is unquestionably a product of immense coercion. Norms are brutal instruments of social control. Society inflicts them upon us at birth, and they are seldom removed until rigor mortis sets in. Society is a prison or a puppet theater (two of Peter Berger's images). We are either chained to the rules that bind our thoughts, beliefs, and actions—or helplessly manipulated by them. So awesome is this force that Durkheim equated it with belief in God. Men everywhere sense a mysterious power far greater than theirs. According to Durkheim they are mistaken only in assuming that this power is supernatural. It is actually societal. Armed with negative and positive sanctions, with punishments and rewards, society holds us fast and forever in an iron grip that no man can break. To be sure, there are intractable types, people who systematically transgress rules. Durkheim even posits the statistical normality of crime. Not to harbor a certain ratio of lawbreakers would be tantamount to constructing a utopia or an antiutopia such as no group has yet been able to approximate. Durkheim tells us that beyond this unspecified ratio, crime is pathological. He doubts that it can ever be eliminated. What? Not even in a community of saints? No, not even there. For, Durkheim reasons, saints, who are notoriously harsh in judging their own morality, would transform venial offenses into deadly sins. But the quasi-positivist Durkheim dared to go further by asking: What if one could do the impossible and obliterate every infraction of the criminal code? Would that be *desirable*? His answer is decidedly negative. The effort would anyhow be unavailing. What would be required is such massive and Draconian repression that no shred of individuality, spontaneity, autonomy, or independence could survive. If crime is destructive (and today's "crime" may be redefined tomorrow as a praiseworthy or heroic deed), then its extirpation may be achieved only by the concomitant elimination of all tendencies that at present are defined as constructive. Durkheim, a liberty-loving sociologist, found this nightmare morally abhorrent. It also seemed to him to be scientifically inadmissable.

If men are constrained by exterior norms that exist prior to, but are ultimately incorporated in consciousness, then their acts are largely predetermined, and Durkheim believed this to be the case. But he by no means considered the individual to lack self-control. His point of view was much closer to Spinoza or Hegel who sometimes held that freedom consists in the recognition of its nonexistence. To Durkheim, as he developed the idea in his *Rules of Sociological Method,* this meant going back along the chain of causes and effects until we find a point where the action of man may be effectively brought to bear. Basically he admonished us to study the regularities in society; mastering them would be prophylactic. We could protect one another through our ability to predict events and therewith advance toward a higher state of human development. Durkheim was convinced that social phenomena down to the most minute ceremonial detail present an astonishing uniformity; if we learn their nature, it will be possible to control them and free ourselves.

Comte's Positive Sociology

Such was Durkheim's credo, one that does not deeply differ from that of Auguste Comte, who is perhaps best remembered for having advanced a slogan once widely embraced and now generally maligned: *Savior pour prévoir et prévoir pour pouvoir.* (To know in order to predict and to predict in order to control.) The last verb is decisive. That Comte was a reactionary elitist and a forerunner of twentieth-century totalitarianism matters much less on this score than that he regarded his "science of sciences" as a vehicle for mastery of the universe. Human beings, equipped with sociological knowledge, would control the world by which they had previously but needlessly been controlled.

Karl Marx's Determinism

No major sociological theoretician is a hard and consistent determinist. If Comte and the neopositivist Rightists who followed him opted for an expansion of reason, they did so with the ultimate objective of securing or enlarging their capacity for self-determination, for domination of the natural and artificial spheres by which they were surrounded. And the neopositivist Leftists—how do they stand? Why, on precisely the same ground. Consider a handful of famous quotations from the pen of Karl Marx:

> In the social production which men carry on they enter into definite relations that are indispensable and independent of their will; these relations of production correspond to a definite stage of development of their material powers of production. The sum total of these relations of production constitutes the economic structure of society—

the real foundation, on which rise legal and political superstructures and to which correspond definite forms of social consciousness. The mode of production in material life determines the general character of the social, political and spiritual processes of life.[6]

Or hear him again, in the preface to his greatest work, with the same doctrinaire confidence he had displayed in his youth:

Intrinsically, it is not a question of the higher or lower degree of development of the social antagonisms that result from the natural laws of capitalist production. It is a question of these laws themselves, of these tendencies working with iron necessity towards invariable results.[7]

Much later, Friedrich Engels, Marx's solitary friend and life-long collaborator, was to temper the severity of all these definite relations independent of anyone's will, these inflexible determinants, natural laws, iron necessities, and invariable results. He belatedly admitted that constitutive components of the so-called superstructure reciprocally influenced the economic substructure or material basis out of which they were alleged to spring. Engels at last stated in so many words that political, legal, and philosophical ideas, religious systems, dogmas, and theories, and even mental reflexes thereof "also exercise their influence upon the course of historical struggles and in many cases preponderate in determining their *form*. There is an interaction of all these elements in which, amid all the endless host of accidents . . . the economic movement finally asserts itself as necessary." If this is determinism, it is highly qualified, not vulgar, monocausal, simplistic determinism. In the same document, a letter to Joseph Bloch dated September 1890, Engels confesses, "Marx and I are partly to blame for the fact that younger writers sometimes lay more stress on the economic side than is due to it. We had to emphasize this main principle in opposition to our adversaries, who denied it, and we had not always the time, the place or the opportunity to allow the other elements involved in the interaction to come

[6] A *Contribution to the Critique of Political Economy* (New York: International Publishers, 1971), p. 11.
[7] *Das Kapital*, vol. I, p. 13.

into their rights." [8] The Marx who lived long enough to exclaim, "Je ne suis pas Marxiste," may well have had those younger writers in mind. As a young writer himself, he had after all reserved this apothegm for the last of his eleven Theses on the philosopher Ludwig Feuerbach: "The philosophers have only *interpreted* the world differently; the point is to *change* it." Marx can be faulted both for his determinism *and* for his voluntarism. What matters is that he encompassed both of them. Each by itself is indefensible. Prometheus Bound must be complemented by Prometheus Unbound if we are ever to approach an adequate sociological representation of man. Hegelianize the figure if you like: take Marx's determinism as thesis, his voluntarism as antithesis, and you get a complicated combination as the indispensable synthesis with which to apprehend man in society.

Indeed this is precisely what Hegel did. It was very largely what he intended by his frequent invocation of "the dialectic." For instance:

> Wherever there is movement, wherever there is life, wherever anything is carried into effect in the actual world, there Dialectic is at work. . . . We find that the limitations of the finite do not merely come from without; that its own nature is the cause of its abrogation, and that by its own act it passes into its counterpart. We say . . . that man is mortal, and seem to think that the ground of his death is in external circumstances only; so that if this way of looking were correct, man would have two special properties, vitality and—also— mortality. But the true view of the matter is that life as life, involves the germ of death, and that the finite, being radically self-contradictory, involves its own self-suppression. [9]

More succinctly, Hegel asserts that, "The truth of Being and Nothing is the unity of the two, and this unity is Becoming." And Becoming,

[8] Friedrich Engels, "Letter to Joseph Bloch," in *Reader in Marxist Philosophy,* eds. H. Selsam and H. Martel (New York: International Publishers, 1963), pp. 204–6.

[9] From a letter by Hegel to Immanuel Niethammer written in 1821 and quoted in Dirk S. Struik's introduction to *The Economic and Social Manuscripts of 1844* by Karl Marx (New York: International Publishers, 1964), p. 32.

the unity of opposites within a framework of human institutions and associations, provides us in one word with the sociological standpoint. As for Marx, he was never a better Hegelian (nor more of a sociologist) than in 1841 when he received his Ph.D. for a thesis that contrasted the philosophies of Democritus and Epicurus. A Marxist of our time summarizes that thesis by noting that in it, "Marx showed how Democritus, whose atoms moved in a straight line only, constructed a physical theory of strict determinism, whereas Epicurus, who allowed the atoms a slight deviation from the straight line, came to a much fuller world outlook *that allowed freedom as well as determinism.* Thus Epicurus reached out for a full philosophy of life, wider and deeper than that of Democritus." [10] (My italics.)

Fortunately, social science need not depend upon the opacities of Hegelian dialectic to reach similarly sound conclusions. Marx devoted most of his life to the demolition of capitalism. As a professional revolutionist and a tireless theoretician, he felt confident that the class war would come to a head, that "the expropriators would be expropriated," industrial operatives would subdue the bourgeoisie —even as the bourgeoisie had overcome the feudal aristocracy—and that they would disestablish the old order. Workers animated by class consciousness in advanced capitalist countries were already in a secessionist mood. Soon, Marx and Engels proclaimed in *The Communist Manifesto* (very soon, for the year of its issuance, 1848, was a tumultuous one, and that was "no accident," as they might have said), any minute now, the old order would be disestablished. Workers of the (Western) world were about to lose their chains. They, the proletariat, with a little help from disaffected intellectuals, could not but be the vehicle of Communist revolution.

We are only too familiar with this scenario. Can anyone but a fanatical sectarian fail to see how poorly it fits our world in the last quarter of a tense and troubled century? Marx was a bad prophet. Peasants, those "rural idiots" Marx so despised, turned out to have prepared the soil most adequately for a "Socialist" revolution that proletarians have yet to manufacture. "Barbarously backward" peo-

---

[10] Struik, Introduction to *Economic and Social Manuscripts*, p. 14.

ples were ripe for what their leaders in a certain segment of the bourgeois intelligentsia termed and still term Marxist revolution. If Marx turned Hegel right side up, as he claimed, then Mao and Castro, among others, have turned Marx upside down. Advanced capitalism did not lead to communism. The remnants of preindustrial feudalism did. All the same, capitalism as Marx, let alone Adam Smith knew it, has all but vanished. About that Marx was right, but mostly for the wrong reasons.

The Persistence of Change in Human Societies

Not that anybody can ever be sure of the "right" reasons. For Marx it was a foregone conclusion that capitalism would go to pieces. Any system with so many inner contradictions could not prevail for long. These contradictions centered on "the relations of production" which, while they increased the physical miseries of workingmen also alienated and unified them. Joseph A. Schumpeter, a broad-gauged economist who freely crossed the frontiers of every social science, also thought capitalism was doomed. A merciless critic of Marx, he concurred in this matter with his formidable predecessor, arriving on common ground by following a path Marx would never have pursued. Schumpeter, writing in the 1940s, finds that capitalism cannot endure because it ". . . inevitably and by virtue of the very logic of its civilization creates, educates and subsidizes a vested interest in social unrest." So begins an excursion into the sociology of intellectuals, or more precisely, people who are not

> a social class in the sense in which peasants or industrial laborers constitute classes; they hail from all the corners of the social world, and a great part of their activities consists in fighting each other and in forming the spearheads of class interests not their own. . . .
>
> Intellectuals are in fact people who wield the power of the spoken and the written word, and one of the touches that distinguish them from other people who do the same is the absence of direct responsibility for practical affairs. This touch in general accounts for another —the absence of that first-hand knowledge of them which only actual experience can give. The critical attitude, arising no less from the in-

tellectual's situation as an outlooker—in most cases also as an outsider —than from the fact that his main chance of asserting himself lies in his actual or potential nuisance value, should add a third touch.[11]

Schumpeter identifies those Greeks of the fifth and fourth centuries B.C. who were known as sophists, philosophers, and rhetors with modern intellectuals. Ancient civilization gave them limited scope. The Middle Ages were only a little more favorable. Forerunners of the current genus intellectual, mostly monks, had access to no more than an infinitesimal part of the population—very few of whom knew how to read and write. The monastery, with its clerks, hatched medieval intellectuals; but capitalism gave them their greatest boon, the printing press. With Gutenberg's invention, "the scribbling set" or *hommes des lettres,* finally came into their own. Thenceforth they could transmit and diffuse messages simultaneously through the whole of Christendom to ever larger numbers of people. Lay intellectuals materialized as humanists, and humanists were primarily philologists who, however, "quickly expanded into the fields of manners, politics, religion and philosophy." Their influence was corrosive. They undermined one social order, helped to beget another, and then set about scuttling it.

No doubt Schumpeter exaggerated the importance of intellectuals as Marx overstated that of his highly idealized proletariat. Each man understood that capitalism generates forces that in the end destroy it. Schumpeter referred to this propensity as "creative destruction." Neither he nor Marx considered the proposition that such a tendency is present *at all times and in every society.* Hence, a sociologist would have to adjudge them as analysts of a concrete case who failed to draw the general inference with which they helped to equip us. Within every human collectivity "a vested interest in social unrest" arises, whether or not it is stimulated by intellectuals. The scribbling set may well have passed its peak. Marshall McLuhan already writes, in book after book, of our nonlinear, postliterate, or electronic age. Others speak with even more reason of postindustrial man. Automation and cybernation cut so deep a swath in economically advanced

[11] Joseph A. Schumpeter, *Capitalism, Socialism, and Democracy* (New York: Harper and Row, 1942), p. 147.

countries that the proletariat constantly shrinks but without Marx's increasing "immiserization." Only the specific forces, and with them the specific velocity, of change differ from one era to the next.

A great deal of what we do in relating to one another is patterned. Much else, a variously smaller or larger part, is unpatterned. Like good and bad, order and disorder are firmly stitched into the fabric of human society. This every seminal sociologist, including Max Weber (or Max Weber above all), has taken for granted. Only the collective traumata of a turbulent era have shaken us back into widespread recognition of this insight. Like the shattered image of man himself, it is incidentally the insight by which sociology stands or falls.

For Further Consideration

1. What is the viewpoint of "classical sociology"?
2. What, according to the author, is the relationship of sociology to:
    a. psychology
    b. political science
    c. economics
    d. philosophy
    e. natural science
    f. norms
    g. determinism
    h. intellectuals

Sociology came into being at a time of rapid and violent social change. It was born in the hot lava of a volcano whose twin craters were the Industrial Revolution and the French Revolution. That volcano, which erupted with such suddenness, soon engulfed everything in its path. It remains alive and active. Quiescent periods, even decades of relative tranquility, merely punctuate a prolonged crisis. Accumulated volcanic ash momentarily signifies a burnt-out state; new ferment produces more flux that gathers even greater momentum. Communities disintegrate, landmarks disappear, traditions dissolve. Nor is any surcease from the relentless decomposition yet to be expected. For the past several centuries, change of unparalleled intensity and phenomenal velocity has simply unsettled mankind.

Some sociologists, partial heirs of the Enlightenment, welcomed wholesale change, but they had an ideal, a redemption, or a utopia fully in view. Few foresaw that modernity amounted to permanent revolution. The majority of learned Europeans who established sociology wished to help restabilize a society they saw collapsing all

2
Social Order
and Disorder

too spectacularly before their eyes. With every brief interlude of peace, and precisely to account for that respite, sociology hatches theories of social order. When the race—this time, to possible thermo-nuclear oblivion—resumes, those theories are superseded by theories of social change. They yield in turn and once again to the rage for order. How to restore stability becomes the overriding question.

In the first flush of grand, or grandiose, sociological thought, Henri de Saint-Simon and his renegade disciple, Auguste Comte, contrived schemes by which they hoped to reduce endemic friction and foster universal harmony. A world going to pieces needed social and spiritual repair. Accordingly, the Saint-Simonians formed a little religious sect that survives to this day. Comte's last delusion, that he would be High Priest in the Religion of Humanity, proved to be a still greater fiasco. Unlike the "scientific socialism" of Karl Marx and Friedrich Engels, sociology failed to attract a devout and faithful following. Comte's successors gained acceptance not as clergymen but as handymen. Unable to produce the millennium, they were sought out to tinker with social problems—at just that juncture in human history when much of the species experienced life itself as a problem. Thus in 1928 Max Scheler, a German philosopher, captured the quintessential function of sociology by exclaiming:

> In the ten thousand years of history, ours is the first age in which man has become utterly and unconditionally "problematic" to himself, in which he no longer knows who he is, but at the same time *knows that* he does not know. It is only by a firm resolution to wipe the canvas clean of all traditional answers . . . and to look upon man with a radical, methodological alienation and astonishment that we can hope to gain some valid insights.[1]

Scheler dolefully articulated our situation in the first third of this century. More than forty years later, it looks much the same—only more so. We have certainly not grown less problematic to ourselves. Neither has the need for methodological alienation and astonishment appreciably declined. Moreover, some usable insights are available to us. None points the way to salvation, but a few do help us grasp our world and cope with it a little bit better. That little

[1] *Man's Place in Nature* (New York: Noonday Press, 1962), p. xii.

bit is all a problem-centered discipline can promise, but with "everything" problematic, it might serve us in good stead.

Power and Consent

Suppose we consider the applicability of a "paradoxical" insight to historical and social problems, some of which greatly agitate the American public at this moment. The insight is venerable, lucid, and simple: *power does not lie exclusively in the hands of those officially authorized to use it.*

Power is usually defined as decision making. We speak of a patriarchal family system as one in which the father rules supreme. Unquestioning obedience to a chief reveals the locus of tribal power. Indexes to corporate power are the table of organization and the pyramidal hierarchy according to which duties and responsibilities are allocated in a company, a church, an army, a club, a university. Who/Whom? was V. I. Lenin's formula for measuring power relations. Decoded, the formula reads: Who does what to whom? Who decides? Who, having decided, enjoys the capacity to make others obey whether or not they want to? Armed with these and collateral questions (Who runs this town? Who heads up this agency? Who is chairman of the board or of the party? Who is president of the lodge? Of the secret society? Of the nation-state?)—the investigator sets out to identify a ruling class, an establishment, an elite, or a power structure. On this basis, for example, C. Wright Mills could describe what he took to be the American power elite. Mills reasonably assumed that whoever makes those decisions that affect the greatest number of other people has the greatest power over them. On that basis, he spelled out the American power elite as a mixture of men (without women) occupying key positions in government, business, and the armed forces. The careers of such men frequently overlap. They move easily from one category to another, e.g., from military to political to commercial or financial occupations. Their schooling and their tastes range from similar to identical. They constitute an interlocking, multicellular colossus that bestrides American society.

So much meets the eye. At most, it tells half the story. The other half or more is implicit in words like *agreement, consent,* and *cooperation.* The power relationship, like all forms of social interaction, is mutually determined. Crushed, compelled, coerced, the subordinate party can yet withhold compliance. Authority, which descends from above, is checked from below. The absolutely one-sided imposition of will does not exist. A given social organization would collapse, as now and then it does, when enlisted men defy their superior officers, when workers turn a deaf ear to their bosses, when children rebel against their parents. An exchange of influences, a complex reciprocity is always at work. Global management or total control by power holders cannot be sustained. Those in power may be the first to discover how powerless they really are. The chief executive of a mighty state such as our own, his prepresidential illusions notwithstanding, quickly learns that "the people" are an intractable lot. More than that, the tyrant, with supposedly unlimited political muscle at his disposal, needs to reckon with incalculable expressions of protest. Decades ago Georg Simmel set forth this idea with systematic brilliance. At present its assimilation evokes astonishment only among those who are unprepared to acknowledge the margin of freedom that is forever at their fingertips. Simmel declared, "All leaders are also led; in innumerable cases, the master is the slave of his slaves." In the same famous passage he quotes a German politician who, in referring to his followers, said: "I am their leader. Therefore I must follow them." Simmel continues:

> In the grossest fashion, this is shown by the journalist. The journalist gives content and direction to the opinions of a mute multitude. But he is nevertheless forced to listen, combine and guess what the tendencies of this multitude are, what it desires to hear and to have confirmed, and whither it wants to be led. While apparently it is only the public which is exposed to *his* suggestions, actually he is as much under the sway of the *public's* suggestion.[2]

The element that appears to be wholly passive is actually hyper-

[2] This quotation and those that follow from Weber, Mills, Gerth, Bierstedt, and Barnard will be found, sequentially organized, in Chapter 5, "Power and Authority," in *Sociological Theory,* 3d ed., eds. Lewis A. Coser and Bernard Rosenberg (New York: Macmillan, 1969), pp. 133–86.

active, mutually spontaneous forces come into play, action on the part of authorities elicits reaction. The guided mass is far from inert. It is not purely receptive. Simmel even brings to bear the testimony of a hypnotist that in every hypnosis the hypnotist is affected by the hypnotized, and that this mutuality is essential to the hypnotic state. Less extreme examples are the speaker and his audience or the teacher and his class. Groups composed of no more than two people, as well as those that encompass large numbers of men and women, function in accordance with the same principle of give and take. A power elite unresponsive to the underlying population, or seriously contravening its felt needs, cannot endure. Such an establishment invites disestablishment. Youngsters who have shaken the foundations of society while theoretically under total control by their elders, intuitively grasp the validity of Simmel's insight.

Legitimacy, Authority, and Power

Neither would these youngsters find it difficult to follow Max Weber's search for the bases of legitimacy which all ruling powers, "profane and religious, political and apolitical," claim for themselves. The claim to legitimate power and concomitant acquiescence before its majesty are insupportable unless a majority of subjects, citizens, or underlings recognize and embrace that claim. As members of an association who comprise the "underlying" population, they give their loyalty to an official or to the office he occupies. Weber classified authority into three conceptually distinct models or "ideal types." Of these the newest and commonest is the _legal_ type, which rests on rationally established rules. Exercising his power more as a trustee than as a person, the official knows that his area of jurisdiction is functionally circumscribed. Both he and those subject to his directives are bound by statutory regulation. In bureaucratic administration the impersonal rule is decisive. But the rule conveys no sanctity. Its renegotiation, reinterpretation, modification, or nullification are never precluded. The result is a kind of bureaucratic rule with democratic underpinnings in which private favor and personal privilege are minimized.

A second and historically more important type of authority was denominated by Weber as *charismatic*. It goes back to the widely held conviction that a specific person is supernaturally endowed with extraordinary qualities. The governed submit to this person, be-he a sorcerer, a prophet, a dictator, a chieftain in war, or a leader of the hunt, solely because they believe in his magical powers. The charismatic aura he radiates must be enlarged by revelations and inspirations, by miracles, victories, and general successes with no notable interruption, which the governed construe to be broadly beneficial. Neither rational nor traditional norms apply to charismatic authority, which, therefore, is inherently revolutionary in the sense that it is not tied to the status quo. Hence Jesus Christ, the charismatic leader par excellence, typically addresses his adherents: "It is written [thus and so]—but I say unto you . . . !"

The charismatic leader validates himself by repeatedly inspiring awe and wonder. Through divination and revelation, he is able to act as an innovator. Once his work is done, after he has dealt successfully with an emergency or affected a change and destabilized the status quo, improvisation comes to an end. If the charismatic ruler dies, his magic is buried with him. A struggle for the succession ensues. No matter what means are used to resolve the struggle (such as apostolic or hereditary succession, in which the ruler is consecrated by sacramental substantiation), new or old rules, conventions of some kind, must be reinstituted. With their return, routinization, rationalization, and traditionalization have crystallized.

Traditionalism is Weber's third type of authority. He defines it as an attitude that hallows workaday routine. Long-established procedures are viewed as inviolable for no other reason than that they have "always existed." Any departure from these practices is an impious act that produces religious and magical evils. To sanctify tradition in this way is typically to accept patriarchal domination: authority stems from the elder, the father, the uncle, the oldest brother, who becomes master, patron, prince, or lord. To him alone is reserved a certain arbitrariness of action by which he judges on a personal rather than a functional basis.

This is not the place to expound Weber's endlessly suggestive analysis in its entirety. For that we would be required to write a separate book. What matters here is Weber's stress on the legitimation of authority. C. Wright Mills, who later took a more superficial view of the American power elite, when writing with his teacher, the Weberian Hans Gerth, echoed an aphorism of Rousseau's: "The strongest is never strong enough to be always master, unless he transforms his strength into right, and obedience into duty," and another assertion to the same effect by a sixteenth-century prelate William Laud, archbishop of Canterbury: "There can be no firmness without law; and no laws can be binding if there is no conscience to obey them; penalty alone could never, can never do it."

N β

Prestige, Influence, Force, and Dominance

Robert Bierstedt provides further elucidation of the same point. His generic concept is social power, of which economic, familial, financial, political, industrial, and military power are specific manifestations. If power relations saturate any community and every society, as they do, then their "primitive base and ultimate locus" cannot be the state. Power is utterly pervasive. It includes but antedates and transcends government power. The term itself is opaque. In his closely reasoned analysis, Bierstedt attempts to show what social power is chiefly by demonstrating what it is not. For instance, power is not prestige. Closely associated at times, they vary independently at other times. Al Capone, who in his heyday as czar of the American underworld is estimated to have been netting $1 million a day, had power of a kind, but no prestige. A childhood recollection of this writer's is having seen Capone's mansion in Florida. I most vividly remember a large slab on which upper-class residents of the neighborhood had inscribed their names. Capone's name was effaced. At the peak of his illicit power, a gangster's prestige—except with other and would-be gangsters—approaches zero. His opposite number, the policeman, similarly has power but little or no prestige. On the other hand, distinguished scientists and artists, an Albert Einstein or a Pablo Picasso, find that they have enormous prestige, but no sociologically significant power. Bierstedt sets aside as components of prestige unaccompanied or incidentally accompanied by power such qualities as skill, knowledge, competence, ability, and eminence.

He likewise differentiates power from influence and dominance. For him, influence belongs on the ideological, and dominance on the psychological plane. Plato, Aristotle, Saint Thomas, Shakespeare, Galileo, Newton, and Kant were men of influence, although all of them were devoid of power. Of Karl Marx, whose thinking has had an incalculable influence on the twentieth century, Bierstedt says: "This poverty-stricken exile who spent so many of his hours immured in the British Museum was hardly a man of power. Even the assertion that he was a man of influence is an ellipsis. It is the ideas which are influential, not the man." By the same token, dominance characterizes interpersonal rather than intergroup relations. Dominance pertains to the individual trait, to role and temperament, and not to the structure of society in which power is embedded. Again, "rights," which are usually a prerequisite of power, should not be confounded with it. One may have a legal or customary right without the power to enforce it.

Mindful of these logically and sociologically persuasive distinctions, we are better prepared for the most salient of them. Once he has cleared the ground, Bierstedt is ready to define power as *latent force*. The predisposition or the prior capacity to use force, and not its actual exertion, spells power. When authorities resort to force, they are engaged in the negation of their power. The noun "power," as Bierstedt points out, has been hypostatized from the adjective "potential." Power, which is nothing if not a symbol, represents the unused ability to introduce sanctions. By definition, then, power cannot fail. To present an unsuccessful threat of force is to lose power. Its continued possession presupposes restraint in a framework of conscious or unconscious checks and balances. Symbiosis typifies the power relationship. Authority is institutional or legitimate power to which people in formal as well as informal organizations and unorganized communities either surrender or, perversely, refuse to surrender. Those clothed in authority have only as much power as subordinates grant, relinquish, yield up, or otherwise convey to them.

By and large they convey a great deal—else a society made up of opposed and unequally powerful groups could not survive at all. Neither widespread obedience nor periodic disobedience is self-explanatory. Gerth and Mills, as authors of *Character and Social*

Structure: The Psychology of Social Institutions, a textbook written in 1953, when academic youth were known as a "silent generation," present the puzzle of conformity. Why do men obey? Are they just like herd animals, led by a strong man who stays out in front? Perhaps, the authors admit, in some primitive societies where physical prowess is exalted, and in the fighting gang where muscle decides leadership, he who is strongest forces obedience from everyone else. But even these illustrations are suspect. Guile, intelligence, dexterity, nepotism, or a gift for conspiracy and skill in psychological manipulation surely matter as much as sheer physical prowess. Biologically enfeebled elders are known to rule their juniors even in primitive warrior tribes. Furthermore, the puny but clever and charismatic boy, with a "Napoleonic complex," has it within him to become the leader of his gang.

It is precisely the incongruity of physical and mental weaklings in charge of strong men that led Gerth and Mills away from overconcern with power holders: "Although Bismarck once said that you can do all sorts of things with bayonets except sit on them, obviously power and obedience involve more than differences in the biological means and physical implements of violence."

Power, Compliance, and Communication

Stable power relations imply a consensus between subordinates and superordinates. Whether taken for granted or elaborately articulated, such a consensus is indispensable. Theorists who made much of "the social contract," "natural law," or "public sentiment," no matter how muddled they may have been, did come close to the crux of the matter. "Conscience," which is to say voluntary obedience, engaged their attention, as it does that of Gerth and Mills. They recognize that coercion by itself will never outweigh the symbols of justification and the need for legitimation without which "duly constituted authority" becomes a hollow shell.

An authority system works effectively when and only when the issuance of orders, commands, and directives is followed by compliant action. No one has enlivened this sociological "law" more resourcefully than Chester Barnard, a businessman and a scholar who will long be remembered for his incisive study, *The Functions of the Executive*. Terence Hopkins has demonstrated how Barnard's reflections converge with and complement Weber's, a fact obscured by their divergent phraseology. Both Weber and Barnard attempted to analyze systems of bureaucratic authority. In large-scale organizations, Weber described a pyramid, with trained experts manning a power structure legitimated by changeable but rational values. The shape of this structure is determined by "a positive relation between the rank of a unit and its power." Barnard focuses more on lateral extension through communications than on vertical extension through "stratified social space." Barnard's imagery suggests a wheel with lines of communication as spokes radiating from the organization's center. Relevant information passes back and forth until it reaches decision makers who, after sifting the facts that come to them, discharge their responsibilities. On the one hand, we have Weber's power structure; on the other, Barnard's network of communication. Also, Weber envisages a rationally organized corporate group, Barnard a formally organized cooperative group. But Hopkins observes the decisive convergence: "Both men . . . see the problem of authority as primarily a problem of compliance, they define compliance in the same general way, and in consequence, their theories are addressed to the same range of problems, the determinants of stable structures of compliant actions." As conceptualized by Weber, authority appears when a given order is obeyed, or in his words, when the recipient's action "follows in essentials such a course that the content of the command may be taken to have become the basis of action for its own sake." Barnard puts much the same proposition in different language. For him, organizational authority exists when a communication from above is accepted, which occurs if the communication governs the recipient's action, determining what "he does or does not do so far as the organization is concerned."

Challenges to Authority

Barnard, as a seasoned executive, pondered the relationship between labor and management. He independently drew conclusions that not only coincide with those of Max Weber, but radically relocate power quite as much as Simmel ever did. Barnard's originality is most striking in his discussion of motives that account for the inferior's willingness to accept his superior's demands. These demands are classified from the recipient's viewpoint. Some of them the subordinate would consider wholly unacceptable; others he would place on the borderline of acceptability; and yet others he would deem unquestionably acceptable. In the last category belong all the orders that we readily or willingly obey. They occupy what Barnard labeled the "zone of indifference." A smoothly functioning social order will have institutionalized that zone to its uttermost extremes. Contrariwise, let a sizable number of people feel that they are being ordered to do things that displease, annoy, or outrage them, and authority crumbles. The power we yield up is always ours to repossess. Well past the zone of indifference, men with a modicum of community support are no longer loath to question authority. They will resist altogether unacceptable demands, lay aside their tools or their arms, sit down, or sit-in. Noncompliance, nonviolent resistance, civil disobedience, plain orneriness, and intractability are the most potent means by which order is transformed into disorder. If faith can move mountains, so can the loss of faith. Accept authority, and you do its bidding. Reject that authority as oppressive or obnoxious, and the powers-that-be are transmuted into the powers-that-were. Deauthorization is the inelegant sociological way of describing what takes place. Leo Tolstoy, Henry David Thoreau, Mohandas K. Gandhi, and more recently Martin Luther King, Jr., explained it all with the passion and eloquence exclusively allotted to visionaries of their stature. Many a humbler man chafing against the bonds that hold him in submission has stumbled upon the same knowledge.

A number of correlative propositions follow from the general principle I have been attempting to summarize. One is that in human affairs a measure of freedom always exists. To be sure, the extreme existentialism sometimes expressed by Jean Paul Sartre and his devotees, who hold that men have unlimited freedom of choice, would seem to be untenable. A moment's sociological reflection is enough to dispel that myth. We do not choose to be born, let alone to be born at this time in this place as, say, white middle-class Anglo-Saxon Protestants. From the moment of birth through every vicissitude that ensues to senescence and death, a heavy weight of constraint presses upon us. Physical and biological nature which, to insure his own survival, man alone has partly subdued, still holds him tightly in its grip. So, too, that second nature that is man-made constrains and coerces us from first to last. The extent and the variety of normative or cultural determination, which prompts us to act in accordance with a body of binding rules we did not contrive, is the stock in trade of sociology. What must be added is that human beings are bound *and unbound* by the same cognitive, expressive, or broadly linguistic and symbolic means by which they lead their separate and uniquely human lives.

Deauthorization and the Loss of Legitimacy

A single sociological insight, i.e., that power does not lie exclusively in the hands of those officially authorized to use it, has taken us this far. We will arrive at a similar terminus by other paths in this book. For the moment, let us return to that insight and briefly sample the uses to which it can be put. First, consider almost at random the work of an historian, in this instance that of C. V. Wedgwood, grappling with the causes of the civil war that turned England into an armed camp during the middle years of the seventeenth century. Wedgwood weighs the dynastic, religious, constitutional, and above all economic aspects of a bloody conflict such as Britain has never experienced before or since its only full-scale revolution. Many other English historians make much of the crown's poverty, King

Charles's financial ineptitude, and Parliament's jealous control of subsidies. Conceding all that, Wedgwood goes on to note about the King:

> It was not lack of money that prevented him from quelling the revolt of the Scots in 1639 and 1640. Twice over, with or without money, he got an army together and marched it to the North. But the spirit was lacking. The men were deplorably bad material: "all the rogues in the kingdom," said Sir Jacob Astley; and they were very unwilling to fight. What undermined the King's policy much more than lack of funds was lack of cooperation. Strafford, the King's chief minister, spoke of "a general disaffection to the King's service." Among those responsible for recruiting, equipping and sending the troops, from Lords Lieutenants to Justices of the Peace, the majority shared in this "general disaffection." They were at worst hostile to the King's policy, at best bored with it, and their behavior varied from the indifferent to the actively obstructive. They had neither faith in nor respect for the King's government.[3]

King Charles had no countrywide civil service, no bureaucratic clique dependent upon him. Royal policy, which he divulged by proclamation, had to be implemented by local gentry, a stratum of gentlemen, principally those accorded the rank of justices, with vested interests and traditions of their own. "If a majority of them felt no enthusiasm for the policies of the Crown, as far as these affected the internal life of the country, then the policies of the Crown could not be carried out." When the crunch came, a majority felt less than the requisite enthusiasm. Like many another monarch, Charles overestimated his power:

> In theory, King Charles understood the necessity of controlling the Justices, who were required to report regularly to the central government. But he failed to realize what Queen Elizabeth had always known, that in practice his powers depended on making his policies acceptable to those who were to enforce them. Thus, when it came to the Scots war, the troops were well aware that the gentry, who had unwillingly scraped them together, were no more interested in the war than they were themselves. Desertion, indiscipline and mutiny followed naturally from this knowledge.[4]

"Wiping the canvas clean of all traditional answers," anyone

[3] C. V. Wedgwood, *The Covert Rebellion* (New York: Macmillan, 1956), p. 87.
[4] Ibid., p. 93.

animated by the sociological spirit is bound to paint a novel picture, etching, sketching, shading, and limning familiar events in an unfamiliar manner. Like all art, which in a way it is, good sociology broadens and deepens our apprehension of reality. No matter where we begin—from however lofty a point in the social scale—sociological sensibility will take us back to the grass roots, to the social undergrowth, without which all else withers and rots. Accordingly, let us touch (no more than once over lightly) on a second historical case in point.

Elwin H. Powell, a sociologist interested in illuminating "the abstract relationship between consensus and coercion," recently undertook an inquiry into the history of Rome. Why the ancient Empire fell is a perennial perplexity to classical historians—not that they have been lacking in ingenious answers. Edward Gibbon, Samuel Dill, Michael Rostovtzeff and a small host of other classical historians, from Tacitus to Stringfellow Barr, have much to teach us—not only about Rome, but also and unintentionally about the age in which each of them recorded his thoughts. It is unlikely, however, that any earlier chronicler would take quite the tack of a sociologist like Powell. From his bird's-eye view he traces Rome's rise as a dominant Italian city-state, and her expansion and fatal collision with Carthage, which eventuated in the Punic Wars, from whose victorious outcome Rome never recovered. Whenever the Roman Empire resorted to organized terror, that technique subtly undermined whatever stability it temporarily achieved. Powell, drawing upon F. R. Cowell, a contemporary historian of ancient Rome, writes of Spartacus, who led a notable slave revolt, that between 73 and 71 B.C. he assembled an armed force of 120,000 men that defeated many Roman armies. "Finally cornered, Spartacus and his men fought with desperate ferocity until all but 6,000 perished, and these were crucified along the whole road from Capua to Rome—about 60 miles." Powell comments: "Crucifixion was used as a deterrent: through terror the Romans maintained public order *but destroyed the basis of all positive allegiance to the social system.*" [5] (My italics.) Gibbon, who took a dim view of Christianity,

---

[5] Elwin H. Powell, "Anomie and Force: The Case of Rome," *Catalyst* (Spring 1969), p. 80.

would no doubt have agreed that crucifixion was an equally efficacious deterrent to the triumph of a new world religion.

Aware of the Roman Republic's fall from "cohesion to chaos," and of the Roman Empire's lapse from "order to alienation," Powell is most interesting on the Punic Wars. Cato the Elder, then an eighty-three-year-old senator, strongly advocated total annihilation of the Carthaginians. The equally respected Scipio pleaded for "coexistence" or "détente." The emperors accepted Cato's strategy, without which they felt that Rome would not be safe and secure. "Carthage was destroyed but Rome never recovered." Spartacus and Cato were symbolic prefigurations of the downfall to come.

Besieged as a haven of refuge, Rome in the beginning attracted citizens and allies. Hers was then a "policy of prudent generosity." The idea of fair play, the rule of law, the notion of justice more than any other single component lent luster to Roman civilization. They are substantially what Western man must mean when he speaks of the grandeur that was Rome. The abrogation of that grandeur, the substitution of force for law in civil life and in external affairs, produced intolerable strain and strife. Usurpation and assassination replaced orderly rule as generals—Marius, Sulla, Pompey, and Caesar—seized the imperial power they could not hold. Treachery, conspiracy, suspicion, and distrust, the "hate" Rostovtzeff regarded as immeasurable, caused Romans "utterly to lose their balance." Rostovtzeff tells us in his history of the Roman Empire that chaos and misery reigned through the empire while "terror and compulsion . . . gradually developed into a more or less logically organized system of administration."[6] Surveying the social wreckage wrought by desperate emperors, Jakob Burckhardt, a nineteenth-century Swiss historian, concluded that they were not especially ambitious or malevolent men. Without any apparent planning or marked lust for personal power, in the third century A.D. the emperors had created "a slave state with a small ruling minority headed by an autocratic monarch, who was commander of an army of mercenaries." Burckhardt did not believe that the monstrosity they produced corresponded to their ideal. Rather he

---

[6] Michael Rostovtzeff, *The Social and Economic History of the Roman Empire* (New York: Oxford University Press, 1957), p. 449.

assumed the emperors took it to be the best or easiest way of preventing a final breakdown. And this too was a gross miscalculation. Samuel Dill, for whom the fall of Rome was "a tragedy in the truest sense," saw an inexorable fate at work, in which, "The claims of fancied omnipotence ended in humiliating paralysis." [7]

Was the fall of Rome a Greek tragedy? Were the heroic protagonists mere playthings of the gods? Or is a gifted American poet, Robert Lowell, closer to the mark when he writes of "The state, if we could see behind the walls/is woven of perishable vegetation"? These lines appear in a poem entitled "Stalin." Lowell asks:

> Stalin? What shot him clawing up
>   the tree of power—
> millions plowed under like the crops
>   they grew,
> his intimates dying like the spider-
>   bridegroom?

Our answer is that "perishable vegetation" behind Kremlin walls had much to do with it. The psychopathic brute, whether Stalin or Hitler—or Caligula—flourishes only so long as a good deal of social vegetation permits him to satisfy his blood lust. When the populace wavers, madmen vested with authority destroy their power. They do so most dramatically by recourse to unbridled force, to what Simmel called the Law of the Lion, to the Carthaginian solution, the Catonic rather than the Scipionic strategy. Hence Powell's summary passages on Rome would seem to be wholly justified. Referring to the penultimate stages of decay, Powell holds that:

> Because there was no principle of legitimacy and cohesion and no opportunity for participation in political life terror was increasingly used to control the population. Direct violence kept the slave population in tow; the indirect and vicarious violence of the gladiatorial game engendered cowardice and subservience in the free population. Slaves and proletarians constituted 90 per cent of the population; the small upper class lived a functionless and parasitical existence which left it aimless, demoralized and cruel. [8]

And then, "Unable to 'legitimate' the violence which it unleashed,

[7] Quoted by Powell in "Anomie and Force," p. 96.
[8] Ibid., p. 101.

the Roman Establishment was finally undermined by massive defection and desertion. Unable to maintain order despite overwhelming physical force, the Roman Empire collapsed and died an unmourned death." [9]

Deauthorization in Contemporary Society

Sociology is a constant quest for uniformities in social action. Its practitioners should be able to form a generalization in accordance with the accepted canons of logic, which would read: under certain conditions, "if A, then B"—qualified only by a specifiable degree of probability. Thus if subordinates acquiesce to the rule of authority, then and only then can it function effectively. The reverse follows: any considerable disinclination to acquiesce and cooperate illegitimizes or disestablishes authority. We have need for both sides of this coin. They not only reflect molar and molecular conduct at two extremes—that of relative stasis and that of inordinate turmoil— but various intermediate types as well. A continuum could be constructed that would enable us to place actual situations at some point within its confines. Our current situation would veer sharply toward inordinate turmoil. The pervasive crisis of confidence, not yet as grave as that which afflicted seventeenth-century England or Imperial Rome in its senescence, is still very real and variously acute in every part of the world. Wherever we look, the crisis is manifest.

As this is written, many youngsters are rebellious not only in New York or New Haven, but in New Delhi, London, Tokyo, Berlin, Buenos Aires, Jakarta, Cairo—almost everywhere. A decade ago the problem would have been to explain their docility. Quite suddenly, the generation gap, which has never been completely absent, has widened to such proportions that internal discord begins to match if not to outstrip international strife. A sexual revolution, a drug culture, with beats, hippies, delinquents, Teddy boys, stilyagis in Russia, militants, provos in Holland, separatists, and communitar-

[9] Loc. cit.

ians, materialized virtually overnight. Their spokesmen repudiated
the whole spectrum of values handed down to them. In the economically developed European and North American countries, rebellious youth objected to materialism. They took special exception to
"the consumer culture" of their progenitors. Formal democracy with
constitutional safeguards? A sham. Civil rights and civil liberties?
Bourgeois hypocrisy. The university? A cloak for the machinations
of military-industrialists. The list is long. It constitutes an exhaustive
bill of particulars, a total indictment. In addition, extremists relegated anyone over thirty to oblivion.

A parallel eruption of discontent, fostered for awhile by the
state in China, opposed everywhere else, appeared in the economically less developed countries. The immemorial Chinese clan having already evaporated in Communist China, smaller family units
came under systematic attack. Mao Tse-tung unleashed teenage
Red Guards to assault his own not so firmly established administrators, presumably to reinvigorate the revolution. For a full year he
saw to it that every school in his domain was shut tight. His sayings
made up the extraacademic curriculum. They were chanted by
young Maoists around the world. In Africa "progressive" leadership
of whatever ideological color vigorously pursued detribalization—
only to invite further generational conflict. In the captive nations of
Eastern Europe, in Bucharest, in Prague, in Budapest, in Zagreb,
even in Moscow and Leningrad, student protest made itself felt.
Communist youth presented the reverse image of capitalist youth.
Eastern European students demanded "all the good things" like academic freedom, a higher standard of living, autonomous trade
unions, and formal democracy—which had grown stale and distaste-
ful to the Western rebels.

Nowhere are adults more offended and bewildered by riotous
student unrest than in the United States. Like the unrest of women,
of dark-skinned minorities, of the poor, of the lower middle class,
of the New Left and the Radical Right, student unrest confronts a
respectable and once complacent citizenry in whose members it
generates more shock, dismay, and anger than understanding. And
who can help being puzzled at such a spectacle? The richest, in
many respects freest, technologically most advanced people on earth

are also more unstable than anyone predicted—or dreamed—but a little while ago. A sizable number of students who since the republic was founded have known that they could confidently look to privileged positions in American society choose instead to opt out of it. Higher (and lower) learning are in jeopardy. Sanctions fail. The riptide, fed by racial tension, carries a powerful undertow that threatens to overwhelm all orderly arrangements. Thoughtful observers, jittery officials, and worried parents wonder what to do.

Simplistic solutions abound. Modern medicine men hawk their nostrums on every street corner. The sociologically informed can do no more than contribute their smidgin of insight to what they must insist is an enormously complicated situation. If we can shed one ray of light on parts of that situation, something has been accomplished. David K. Cohen does so in a recent issue of *Commentary* magazine. Cohen is a professor attached to the Harvard School of Education. He addresses himself to the cry for decentralization and community control of public schools where every type of racial disparity has been deemed injurious to underprivileged children. His overall assessment is deeply pessimistic—for many reasons it would not now be pertinent to explore. The sociological relevance of his analysis consists in this, that he perceives:

> . . . a profound *crisis of authority* in ghetto schools, *a sense that these schools lack legitimacy* as educational institutions. This feeling is strongest among Negroes—especially the young, the activists and the professionals—but it is reinforced by the many middle- and upper-middle-class whites who reject the public schools' regimentation and authoritarianism for other reasons. For some blacks and whites, the notion that only parents and community residents are legitimately empowered to operate schools rests on what is taken to be the objective inadequacy of those in authority: scarcely anyone with access to print denies that the schools have failed to correct ghetto educational problems. Repeated for years, this assertion has led effortlessly to the idea that the established agencies lack the special competence upon which most educational authority is assumed to rest. (My italics.)[10]

By and by, whenever and wherever confidence in any institutional complex falters, a condition of palpable vulnerability sets in,

[10] "The Price of Community Control," *Commentary* 48, no. 1:28.

and the seal of legitimacy is erased. The erosion of authority cannot be successfully countered by penalties, punishments, and other sanctions. Ghetto resentment has gone beyond the point where inner-city schools can be forced to remain as they have been. Similarly, college and university administrators who hope to preserve the old academic order by tough tactics will find that they are in a hopeless bind. An organizational transformation is unavoidable. The old order presumed a certain willingness on the part of all concerned to preserve rational discourse and free inquiry. Once that tacit social contract has been deeply breached, its basis is also extinguished. Now the college president and his board of directors discover that when a campus is disrupted, they have hardly any options. If their response is conciliatory, it may cause student leaders to make further and, in their eyes, unfulfillable demands. Granting the most extreme demands for student power guarantees destruction of the traditional university, with all its positive and negative qualities. The American public is not likely to allow such an outcome. Alternatively, if strikes and riots paralyze the college, its officials can call upon police power. They may petition for new laws, seek court injunctions, or failing all else, ask for military intervention. By such Draconian means, student rebellion is effectively repressed—and the traditional university ceases to exist. Only another social contract to which neither student body, faculty, nor administration objects can save an institution of higher learning so far gone in tension and discord. And such an institution is a paradigm of all institutions. Human beings as they interact spin a seemingly strong but actually delicate institutional tissue. In a time of trouble like our own, when radical dislocation is perceptible to everyone, the tissue which breaks cannot easily be put together again. It was cemented with an ever-so-soluble trust. Distrust and suspicion, nowadays called credibility gaps, are incompatible with social order. In the long run, "projective distrust," generalized hostility, the growth of suspicion and concomitants thereof (the fear of being used, the sense that "someone" is pulling the strings, a devil theory) exacts a heavy political price. Very often it turns into abject dependence. In this context, Herbert Blumer has surely expressed the better part of sociological wisdom, as follows:

Oddly, the most effective restraint on the exercise of power is the calculation of the losses that might be sustained through its use in given situations. Power action, by definition, encounters resistance and is subject to assessment by opposing groups who seek in their own interest to locate its points of weakness and vulnerability. Thus its use and extension are subject to the limitations of possible failure, of exceeding its potential, of encountering the risks of unsustainable loss. . . . Without this self-correction, power struggle would attain the unrestrained viciousness which is usually and unwarrantedly ascribed to it.[11]

For Further Consideration

1. What social conditions gave rise to sociology as a separate discipline?
2. Where does the locus of power in society lie?
3. What is the relationship of power to consent?
4. (a) What is meant by the term legitimacy?
   (b) What are the major types of legitimacy? Define each.
5. What are the relationships between power and prestige?
6. How is power defined? What are its major forms?
7. (a) What is meant by deauthorization?
   (b) How does the author illustrate the concept?
8. What is the relationship between coercion and consent?
9. What are the evidences for the idea that contemporary society is being deauthorized?

[11] Herbert Blumer, "Social Structure and Power Conflict," in *Industrial Conflict,* eds. Arthur Kornhauser et al. (New York: McGraw-Hill, 1954), p. 236.

Cultural Contradictions

OVER thirty years ago, Robert S. Lynd, the celebrated coauthor of two community studies, *Middletown* and *Middletown in Transition,* published his third book, *Knowledge for What?* Today much of it seems too ephemeral and tendentious to bear serious rereading. Here and there, however, the book is startlingly topical, and nowhere more so than in a fourteen-point list of outstanding American assumptions. For the most part, Lynd presents these assumptions as paradoxes or cultural contradictions, strophe followed by antistrophe. Here are a few examples:

Everyone should try to be successful.

But: The kind of person you are is more important than how successful you are.

Life would not be tolerable if we did not believe in progress and know that things are getting better. We should, therefore, welcome new things.

But: The old tried fundamentals are best; and it is a mistake for busybodies to try to change things too fast or to upset the fundamentals.

3
Contradictions in the Operation of Society

Hard work and thrift are signs of character and the way to get ahead.

But: No shrewd person tries to get ahead nowadays by just working hard, and nobody gets rich nowadays by pinching nickels. It is important to know the right people. If you want to make money, you have to look and act like money. Anyway, you only live once.

Honesty is the best policy.

But: Business is business . . .[1]

To assemble a much longer list of incompatible assumptions is today the easiest of tasks. Idealistic adolescents do it all the time in their vain effort to establish a moral consistency that does not exist. The final irony is perhaps that they too are the children of their time and place. Even the most rebellious of them, those who strive to create a separate youth culture, are inescapably caught up in logical and sociological incompatibilities. Repelled by violence, they have recourse to it. Turned off by publicity, with its manipulative mass media, they and their heroes may exploit television to the hilt. While promoting participatory democracy, their organizations become authoritarian. Rejecting "conformity," they fall prey to it.

The American Dilemma

The majority of Americans see our society today as one full of contradictions. And so, most emphatically, are they seen and scorned by their critics abroad. The definitive work on race relations in the United States was written in the forties, and revised recently, by a great Scandinavian scholar, Gunnar Myrdal. He called his encyclopedic work *The American Dilemma*. Myrdal surveyed the American creed as enunciated in our sacred political literature, the Declaration of Independence, the Constitution, the Bill of Rights, and related documents. None condones oppression; all proclaim equality. Yet nearly from the beginning, in institutionalized slavery and after its abolition, white men have oppressed those they took to be their

[1] Robert Lynd, *Knowledge for What?* (Princeton, N.J.: Princeton University Press, 1939), pp. 60–62.

racial inferiors. Thus the American creed is piously affirmed and systematically subverted.

Myrdal, an enlightened man of his time, optimistically concluded in 1944 when he originally set forth our dilemma, that it would have to be resolved quite soon. He duly noted unmistakable signs of improvement in the status of Negro Americans. Ten years later his expectation that the American creed would be fully translated into action seemed to be vindicated, for in 1954 the Supreme Court of the United States ordered desegregation of the public schools. It struck down an insupportable doctrine, that of separate but equal facilities, and cited Myrdal's work to support that decision. To all intents and purposes, the dilemma was about to be resolved, at least with all that "deliberate speed" the Court had enjoined. This illusion persisted through the early sixties as new laws and judicial decisions with legislative effect banished one barrier to racial integration after another. From that point to this, disenchantment, bitterness, tension, and black-white conflict have grown at such a rate that their divisiveness has produced more racial polarization than we have ever before experienced in this century.

Was Myrdal, for all his meticulousness and thoroughness, simply too naïve? Clearly he overestimated the good faith, or the capacity, or the disposition, or the willingness of white America to share democratic rights and privileges with black America—which continued to be separate (even growing separatist) and unequal. Perhaps Myrdal's analysis was too simplistic. By 1949, the prominent American sociologist, Robert K. Merton, thought it was. In that year he submitted a formidable critique of Myrdal.

Merton complicated the stark picture that Myrdal had drawn. He questioned the view that we were confronted merely with a monolithic creed on the one hand and institutional evasion on the other. So to look at the American dilemma was to lose sight of a useful distinction between attitudinal or affective and behavioral or active levels. To be prejudiced (from the French *préjugé,* a judgment made before and irrespective of personal contact) is to harbor an emotion, a feeling, a state of mind. We properly speak of a prejudiced attitude, a mind-set, psychic hostility, and generalized contempt felt by whites toward every member of another ethnic group, in this case Negroes—or blacks or Afro-Americans, as many nonwhites now prefer to be known. No necessary connection links attitude to action. Furthermore, the attitude itself is volatile, more fixed than mixed in certain individuals, but usually ambiguous.

Action based on prejudice is discrimination. And some action not based on prejudice is discrimination. In other words, as Merton asked us to note, prejudice and discrimination need to be distinguished not only for analytical purposes, but also because they may and often do vary independently. By separating the attitudinal from the behavioral dimensions, Merton was able to construct one of his famous fourfold tables. By variously combining his dimensions, he derived the following typology of ethnic prejudice and discrimination. It is vastly more subtle than the obvious juxtaposition of lip-service-to-beliefs and their infringement in actual conduct.

		Attitude Dimension:* Prejudice and Nonprejudice	Behavior Dimension:* Discrimination and Nondiscrimination
Type I:	Unprejudiced nondiscriminator	+	+
Type II:	Unprejudiced discriminator	+	−
Type III:	Prejudiced nondiscriminator	−	+
Type IV:	Prejudiced discriminator	−	−

* Where (+) equals conformity to the creed and (−) deviation from the creed.

This paradigm has its uses.[2] Merton explored several of them to our general edification. For example, he found that Types I and IV were composed of people respectively labeled all-weather ethnic liberals and all-weather ethnic illiberals. Whatever their other quandaries and failings, they could not logically be said to suffer from the American dilemma. All-weather liberals both accept the American creed and act in accordance with its precepts. All-weather illiberals reject the creed out of hand and act with perfect consistency in

[2] See "Discrimination and the American Creed" in *Discrimination and National Welfare,* ed. R. M. MacIver (New York: Harper and Row, 1949), pp. 99–126.

discriminating against those they scorn as inherently inferior to *but could be vexed by behavior of others* themselves.

The dilemma is real—and as such, a possible source of grave personal vexation—only to Types II and III. To be sure, it is precisely these types who make up an overwhelming majority of the white population. They are representative types: men and women who have been socialized to respond appropriately under given circumstances but not so oversocialized that they are unable to respond appropriately under different or even opposite circumstances. Only the *rara avis* who has fully internalized democratic ideals or one who has deeply absorbed their antithesis, will everlastingly live and willingly die for them.

We are indebted to Merton for the conceptual elegance with which he refined and elaborated Myrdal's original statement of our most agonizing social problem. The restatement is invaluable for classificatory purposes, and not to be lightly dismissed as such. Yet, with the wisdom of hindsight, we must fault Merton on at least two scores: (1) he overlooked certain salient theoretical implications in his own analysis, and (2) he therefore fell prey to Myrdal's error (which, be it admitted, virtually all liberals, regardless of skin color tended to share), namely that racial amity would soon prevail in America. How so? By good will implemented in progressive legislation, judicial interpretation, and benevolent administration. It was thought that this consummation would finally elevate a persecuted minority into first-class citizenship.

Merton and most of the rest of us assumed twenty-five, or even ten years ago, that legal rectification of a gross social injustice was at least a feasible alternative to the old American dilemma. Civil rights meant equal rights and eventual integration of white and black America. The law was to be our instrument. With it we hoped to attain ends that most of the population were assumed to cherish. Our reasoning, translated into Mertonian terms, went approximately like this. For those who lived the creed they preached, the all-weather ethnic liberals, law would be superfluous. That type, while still small, was growing rapidly if only because many people enjoyed the benefits of higher education which, in turn, appreciably reduced bigotry. Type II encompassed whites who were not prejudiced but who, in defiance of their own convictions, did discriminate. The fair-weather ethnic liberal is to be found in various guises: a northerner in what used to be the Old Confederacy who abides by local segregationist protocol while chafing inwardly and feeling guilty; an employer who judges his workers by their ability to do a job irrespective of the skin color with which certain gene pools have endowed them, but who feels that he cannot hire blacks without alienating other workers or bigoted customers; a union leader, willing or eager to have a multiracial membership but fearful of losing his post through rejection by a pure white and deeply biased rank and file.

Turn Type II inside out and you have Type III: the fair-weather ethnic illiberal, the southern white racist in liberal northern territory where overtly discriminatory acts are viewed with disfavor; the anti-Negro employer with a liberal constituency that he wishes to hold; the employer whose profits will increase, perhaps in a black ghetto, who, with however many misgivings, liberally hires dark-skinned workers.

A Type IV person is as scrupulously consistent as his opposite number, a Type I person. Under any and all circumstances, he treats people who are, in his eyes, a childish or barbaric abomination with utter contempt and harsh discrimination. Given the depth of his hostility, coupled with a fanatical determination never to yield or compromise, this type alone would evade, circumvent, and sabotage civil rights legislation. Like Myrdal, Merton believed, however, that their numbers were rapidly dwindling and that they would soon be overpowered by the majoritarian will for an ethnically liberal resolution of the American dilemma which had, after all, become an unbearable American tragedy.

So far from disappearing, the dilemma has deepened. To fathom why this should be so would require a separate treatise that we sorely need and that no one has as yet proved capable of writing. Racial discord has caused us to live a spasmodically eruptive, fluid, and violent lie for some centuries and not only in the United States, but all over this hemisphere. Most of us in the 1970s are perhaps as unreasonably depressed about the prospects of achieving racial peace as we were heretofore unreasonably euphoric. It is no reflection on the professional competence or human sensitivity of two such accomplished social scientists as Myrdal and Merton that their prognosis was so wide of the mark. Hardly anyone, certainly not this writer, doubted that they were right. At this moment the dominant mood among expert sociologists is one of profound pessimism. With another turn of the kaleidoscopic scene, with possible amelioration and rectification, that mood may be reversed.

Contradictions between Social Appearances and Realities

I have made this little excursus into the tangled web of American interracial conflict chiefly for illustrative purposes. Such conflict is only the most spectacular example of innumerable social problems that agitate a citizenry in conscious and dangerous turmoil. Still, it differs only in degree and not at all in kind from other problems. *Every society is a living lie.* What are equilibrium and disequilibrium, fixity and change, a normative order and its systematic—or systemic —violation? Surely not a rhythmic procession of successive stages through time and space. In the social structure of mankind, as in nature at large, these artificial dichotomies do not exist. Each of the paired opposites is embedded, enmeshed, and entwined in the other. For every putative social phenomenon, we may safely predicate an underlying and countervailing "noumenon" or cluster of "noumena." Human society is itself necessarily split into two uneven parts, one visible and concrete, the other invisible and intersubjective. Plato's cave is our natural habitation. A little light throws shadows on the wall, and a fragment of that which was previously concealed is briefly revealed, only to be concealed again. The contemporary sociologist Vilhelm Aubert recently wrote of *The Hidden Society* as one in which private perceptions and cognitions predominate. They demand, and Aubert among others attempts to supply at least a preliminary social analysis. Secrecy, deviance, love, sleep (literally the night sight of society and its apparent antithesis), an assortment of supposedly marginal, peripheral, and interstitial states, all fall within his purview. So do choice, chance, creation, transformation, isolation, and the past as an elusive aspect of the present. Aubert writes:

> Society has many agents to deal with the task of making its norms and structures explicit. They define a relevant image of an aspect of society toward which the individual is invited or sometimes forced, to direct his attention. Society continuously describes itself, but never fully, and rarely to the observer. Thus, it is always a task of sociology to reveal the hidden society to its members. . . .[3]

The "Debunking" of Society

Aubert's emphasis, while to some extent original, also bears the earmarks of sociological tradition. In spite of idiosyncrasies and foibles, the fads and fashions to which he is prone, every sociologist worth his salt has found himself revealing, unveiling, or unmasking and debunking the world around him. Those sociologists who focus primarily on their own society, whether they define themselves politically as conservative, radical, or liberal, are bound also to be somewhat subversive. The archconservative, William Graham Sumner, is no less iconoclastic when he points to a constant societal disparity between overt mores and covert morals than is the committed radical, Thorstein Veblen, when he satirizes conspicuous consumption and separates it from the satisfaction of those needs about which economists still write so much. The well-bred reader of Vilfredo Pareto will be as shaken by absorbing one page from Pareto's major work, *The Mind and Society*, as he will be by soaking up a bit of Marx's *Das Kapital*. Pareto, who accepted honors from Mussolini, is in his way as dangerous as Karl Marx, the professional revolutionary. Never mind that Pareto wishes to preserve all "the non-logical residues" that strike him as both laughable and indispensable—while Marx wants them totally extirpated. It does not matter that Durkheim considers religion positively functional if at the same time he strips the sacred sphere of supernatural trappings. The social scientist's message is no different from the natural scientist's or the creative artist's: things are not what they seem to be—appearance does not

[3] *The Hidden Society* (Totowa, N.J.: Bedminster Press, 1965).

faithfully reproduce reality. Once a man has felt the impact of this message, he can never again be the same. The protective layers of belief in which his hereditary social order conspires to encase him will have been removed. Like esthetic sensibility or responsiveness to philosophical inquiry, sociological subtlety breeds skepticism, doubt, rootlessness, and cosmopolitanism.

Learning what the sociologist at his best has to teach is therefore a risky business. It is undoubtedly easier to compartmentalize irreconcilable spheres of everyday life than to recognize and accept them in all their actual contrariety. Men have no great difficulty operating on one level and then on another, first in this manner, afterward in that. Only when the levels are squeezed together, when the peace-loving citizen makes war, when the true believer defiles an altar of his god, is conflict likely to be experienced as a personal problem. Insofar as sociology contributes to an awareness of conflict, it serves to undermine the individual and social order. This is exactly what a so-called conflict theorist like Marx sought to do. He took class conflict to be inherent in and constitutive of antiquity, the Middle Ages, and modern times. Frictionlessness was reserved for a vague socialist paradise of the future. His fondest hope was that prehistoric or primitive communism would at last be restored on a new foundation. Marxists still cling to that hope, but, like their teacher, they acknowledge the need for a subjective commitment to it. The Marxist name for that need is class consciousness. Workers without class consciousness are victims of false consciousness. As such, they are incapable of producing the revolutionary catalyst without which classes cannot be abolished. That Marx fully expected workers to develop a militant, secessionist, and "really" proletarian consciousness is less important than his realization that it was the *sine qua non* for irresistible revolutionary change.

The Universality of Conflict

About Marx or the Marxists of nearly every stripe, none of this is surprising. In an important and less widely appreciated sense, however, it also applies to non-Marxists and even to anti-Marxists, to so-called consensus theorists. They too, implicitly or explicitly acknowledge the universality of conflict. The school called functionalism or structural-functionalism, which for so long held sway over American sociology, did not deny conflict. Its spokesmen tended rather to view conflict as functional. The enormously influential vaticinations of Talcott Parsons, as well as his followers' uncoordinated efforts to operationalize them, have always left a niche, a box, a paragraph, or an afterthought for conflict. Along with change, it was fitted (sometimes tortured) into "the social system" conjured up by Parsons —where everything more or less harmoniously coexists with everything else. No such naïveté can be ascribed to Lewis A. Coser, an American functionalist who in the 1950s and 1960s did give conflict a salient or central position. Coser, less beholden to Parsons than to Simmel, Marx, and Merton, subtly analyzed various situations involving conflict. Some were found to be supportive of the system ("safety valves" which allowed dissident elements harmlessly to let off steam), and others were not. Coser's sophistication in this and all other matters can be taken for granted.[4] But what of Bronislaw Malinowski, the anthropologist who more than anyone else fathered modern functionalism? He is widely dismissed nowadays as an apologist for the status quo, as an ethnographer with conservative bias and therefore, intentionally or not, a lackey of Anglo-British imperialism. Did he not invariably claim that what is, is functional, and thus what is, is right? One's answer to that question has to be negative. Malinowski was no simpleton of the Trobriand Islands.

It was in the Trobriand Archipelago, a group of flat coral islands inhabited by Melanesian tribesmen, that Malinowski did his fieldwork. There he assiduously gathered a wealth of data. It took the better part of a lifetime for him to collate, describe, and interpret his findings. A torrent of publications cascaded from his pen. Among them, none more richly deserves to be read in our time than a monograph originally published in 1926. Its title is *Crime and Custom in Savage Society*.[5] We no longer speak of *savage* society. The word sounds too

[4] Lewis A. Coser, *The Social Functions of Conflict* (New York: Free Press, 1956).

[5] *Crime and Custom in Savage Society* (London: Routledge and Kegan Paul, 1926).

invidious. Even *primitive* society is in semantic disrepute. "Preliterate" (already under some fire) and "nonliterate" are still acceptable. Nothing but this terminological awkwardness dates Malinowski's essay, which is otherwise a marvel of theoretical and substantive relevance. To ponder his data is to dispel many of the illusions fostered by Parsons and a generation of disciples who formalized and desiccated the functionalism they temporarily preempted.

Conflict in Primitive Society

In *Crime and Custom* Malinowski addressed himself to the fundamental issue of social control among nonliterate peoples. Do they follow what "little law they have but fitfully and loosely"? Are they noble savages, free spirits unafflicted as yet by those chains that only civilization forges and fastens on man? Certainly not. The noble savage is an eighteenth-century fiction, propagated by Rousseau in a sustained flight of fancy, welcomed by enlightened despots, royal retainers, and foggy philosophers while being confirmed by missionaries, traders, mariners, and settlers who grossly misunderstood the newly discovered worlds they frequently plundered, developed, and belatedly idealized. Twentieth-century anthropology disconfirmed the naïvely romantic image presented to it by unprofessional observers. An afterimage obtrudes in the ethnography of a Robert Redford or the historiography of Pitirim A. Sorokin—where small, circumscribed familistic folk culture, a "precivilized" and "unspoiled" peasant society replaces the early anthropologist's peculiar pipe dream. Nostalgia for any of many epochs that never existed outside the worshiper's imagination may still provide models for the good and orderly life we allegedly lost in modern times.

By 1926 when Malinowski sat down to write his durable little book, the anthropological ennoblement of nonliterate peoples was much less noticeable than their debasement. The pendulum had swung from one bizarre distortion to another. The savage who was once thought to enjoy an utterly enviable freedom was reassessed as a pathetic creature, bound hand and foot by his devotion to custom, public opinion, and supernatural sanction. In the horde, the clan, and the tribe, individuals were assumed to be passively obedient. The small-scale community makes inviolable demands which nobody dares to defy. So far from being given over to unbridled passion and unfettered excess as creatures of beastly heathen devices, it appeared that primitive men were after all woebegone prisoners of their culture. Every step, every breath they took, not just on ceremonial occasions but in humdrum affairs as well, was subject to firm tribal law. The juridical myth of group-marriage, group-justice, group-property, and group-responsibility begot yet another dogma: the total absence of individual rights and liabilities among nonliterates. If we now realize that no human collectivity, small or large, primitive, folkish, or civilized, operates this way, Malinowski, as much as anyone else, must be thanked for disabusing us.

In one word, he found "savages" to be less than savage—if the epithet is taken to mean either that lawlessness or full, natural, and spontaneous submission to rules is their normal way of life. Instead, a complex hypertrophy of law and custom surrounds the not-so-simple society of people who do not read and write. Some such hypertrophy surrounds every society and is its social surface. We must look most attentively at that surface, which is stocked with more normative variation than the outsider expects. And we must look beneath its beguiling topsoil for the layers of modification and nullification that lurk there.

Malinowski's meticulous study led him to conclude about the average Trobriander that:

> . . . his observance of the rules of law under the normal conditions, when it is followed and not defied, is at best partial, conditional, and subject to evasions; that it is not enforced by any wholesale motive like fear of punishment, or a general submission to all tradition, but by very complex psychological and social inducements. . . .[6]

Again:

> Take the real savage, keen on evading his duties, swaggering and boastful when he has fulfilled them, and compare him with the anthropologist's dummy who slavishly follows custom and automatically

[6] Ibid., p. 15.

obeys every regulation. There is not the remotest resemblance between the teachings of anthropology on this subject and the reality of native life.[7]

As reported by Malinowski, Trobriand law impinges directly on economic, religious, and family relationships. It weaves an intricate network and a delicate tissue of reciprocal obligations, services, and duties, involving constant exchanges and an endless give and take, payment followed by repayment. Primitive jurisprudence, with its unwritten constitution, aims, like our own, at perfect solidarity. And like our own, it is torn by dissension, rivalry, egotism, avarice, exploitation, and crime. "The savage is neither an extreme 'collectivist' nor an intransigent 'individualist'—he is . . . a mixture of both."

Had they but heeded *the* functionalist *par excellence,* how much wiser Parsonian functionalists would have been. Here almost as though Malinowski were admonishing them beforehand for their errors, he exclaims: "It would be a very one-sided picture indeed of the Trobriands, if the rules were shown only in good working order, if the system were only described in equilibrium." This is just the conceptual trap into which too much functionalism fell. Malinowski confronted a primitive system no different in this respect from his and ours. They all function imperfectly, with countless hitches, breakdowns, frictions, and complications.

The most "exotic" feature of Trobriand culture is its separation of biological and sociológical paternity. Descent is traced unilaterally through the mother's line. A father is obligated to look after his sister's children rather than those who have sprung from his own loins. The most important legal principle isolated by Malinowski is that of mother-right, "which rules that a child is bodily related and morally beholden by kinship to its mother and to her only." Matriarchal law governs inheritance, succession, social status, rights to soil, relations between the sexes, local citizenship, and clan membership.

If the principle of mother-right gave Malinowski a master key wherewith to unlock every mystery in one culture, he might well have remained content. With that principle it was possible to expose

[7] Ibid., p. 30.

and anatomize an unfamiliar social system. Not so. Further immersion in the Trobriand culture revealed subsystems and contracultures not unlike those over which we agonize so much in the West.

Having set forth the basic Trobriand system, Malinowski went on:

> But, side by side with the system of Mother-right, in its shadow so to speak, there exist certain other, minor systems of legal rules. The law of marriage, defining the status of husband and wife, with its patrilocal arrangements, with its limited but clear bestowal of author- ity on the man and of guardianship over his wife and children in certain specified matters, is based on legal principles independent of Mother-right, though on several points intertwined with it and ad- justed to it. The constitution of a village community, the position of the headman in his village and of the chief in his district, the privi- leges and duties of the public magician—all these are independent systems.[8]

And therewith we enter the maze of conflicting rules, irreconcil- able civil and criminal laws, incompatible norms, and inconsistent expectations that twists through every human society. The culture that binds men in a normative vise also frees them by requiring that they choose and refuse, that they decide what course to take when their culture provides them with an embarrassment of alternatives.

Malinowski's book suggests nearly as many Trobriand dilemmas, paradoxes, and contradictory assumptions as Lynd lists in his book on our own "hypocritical" America. Actual life and the Trobriander's ideal condition have little in common. Mother-right versus father- love; monogamy and totemic clan exogamy (allowable sexual inter- course and marriage only with someone outside the maternal kinship circle) versus libertinism and incest; magic versus countermagic, a trespass and its institutionalized remedy consisting of spells and rites performed over water, herbs, and stones; a sorcerer's power versus that of another, antipathetic, sorcerer's power; the promulgation of a taboo versus its methodical breach: these are but a few of the diso- nant assumptions detected by Malinowski. They are all immanent sources of strain, generated from within the culture itself. A full picture would include external influence, intercultural in addition to

[8] Ibid., pp. 75–76.

intracultural forces, which at major points of contact jar and mar and seam the fabric of social relations. Quite apart from this order of disruption, a more or less self-contained system, when viewed at close quarters, has to be seen as fractured, divided, alive, mercurial, incapable of absolute fixity, or prolonged stasis and—to that extent —free.

When stern commands are systematically circumvented by well-established methods, Malinowski is surely right that there can be no question of spontaneous obedience to law or slavish adherence to tradition. From the same culture that teaches men to obey without question, men learn how not to obey. If the institution of marriage and the prohibition of adultery are sacred, so is the magic by which to estrange a woman from her husband and induce her to commit adultery. And so is the absolution that may or may not follow. The rationale that goes with contracultural practices is part and parcel of a traditional but only semivisible or quite invisible bundle of subterranean values that must be excavated by the sociologist whenever he seriously digs into his subject.

Early in his first visit to the Trobriands, an event took place that opened Malinowski's eyes to much that he and other fieldworkers had missed. This episode is now and then recounted by American criminologists and by such important students of deviant behavior as Howard Becker. They and we should never lose sight of its implications. In Malinowski's words:

One day an outbreak of wailing and a great commotion told me that a death had occurred somewhere in the neighborhood. I was informed that Kima'i, a young lad of my acquaintance, of sixteen or so, had fallen from a coconut palm and killed himself.

I hastened to the next village where this had occurred, only to find the whole mortuary proceedings in progress. . . .

Only much later was I able to discover the real meaning of these events: the boy had committed suicide. The truth was that he had broken the rules of exogamy, the partner in his crime being his maternal cousin, the daughter of his mother's sister. This had been known and generally disapproved of, but nothing was done until the girl's discarded lover, who had wanted to marry and who felt personally injured, took the initiative. This rival threatened first to use black magic against the guilty youth, but this had not much effect. Then one evening he insulted the culprit in public—accusing him in the hearing of the whole community of incest and hurling at him certain expressions intolerable to a native.[9]

Publicly humiliated, Kima'i the next morning donned festive attire, climbed a coconut tree, spoke from the palm leaves, explaining his "desperate deed," called on clansmen to avenge him for having been driven to it, wailed, bade the community farewell, and plunged to his death. No everyday happening—this, but matched during Malinowski's stay by at least one other nearly identical case of ritual suicide. And the transgression itself, a rather spicy adventure about which native Casanovas were wont to boast, seems to have been about as atypical as premarital and extramarital sex in Western society. Only adolescent indiscretion, open denunciation, and a public scandal, as opposed to gossip and magic, provoked the boy to punish himself for his crime.

That it was a high crime can scarcely be doubted. The prohibition of totemic clan endogamy is one of two or three cornerstones on which Trobriand law and order rest. Without it, mother-right and the intricate structure of kinship would collapse. A breach of the prohibition amounts to incest, and nothing inspires more horror among Trobrianders, or any other aggregation of people we know about, than the thought of incest. Trobrianders told Malinowski they believed sores, disease, and death were the wages of this sin, but Malinowski remarks that it "is the ideal of native law, and in moral matters it is easy and pleasant strictly to adhere to the ideal—when judging the conduct of others or expressing an opinion about conduct in general."

So the fundamental law is violated, and more often than not, it is violated with impunity. Public opinion is not outraged; it must be mobilized by an aggrieved party who hurls insults at the wrongdoer. Even then, shame and not guilt prompts punishment that is self-inflicted. Nowhere in this narrative does Malinowski mention the girl's fate, presumably because it does not deserve comment. The offense required two parties, only one of whom—under very special

[9] Ibid., pp. 77–78.

circumstances—suffered for it. *Sub rosa* affairs of this kind go on all
the time, and when no particular trouble is stirred up, pharisaical
leniency prevails. Without a fixed legal code or an organized means
of administration, suicide, sorcery, and personal vindictiveness partially enforce the biddings of tradition. These devices work approximately as well or as poorly as the people-processing agencies that
handle malefactors in United States society. If Trobriand methods
of meting out punishment are vague, if retribution is uncertain, with
justice subject to chance and passion, while no unalterable institution
exists to assure equal treatment—then, indeed, with all our bureaucratic impersonality, we are right at home in Melanesia. The observ-
able amount of "conventional" crime, murder, theft, and assault, not
to say any real or imagined threat to the prerogatives of an important
personage like a chief or some other notable—all this is evidently as
common on a Trobriand Island as it is on Manhattan Island. Nor does
either have a monopoly on elastic prohibitions joined to methodical
systems of evasion.

If Malinowski finds customary usage nearly as strong as traditional
law, so do we. One may overcome the other, or be subdued by it.
They may collide or work separately, producing a precarious *modus
vivendi* in perpetual motion. Centripetal and centrifugal, convergent
and divergent forces permit a tolerable degree of social cohesion—
and guarantee that it will be gradually or suddenly undermined and
supplanted.

The sociologist then must guard against a propensity he shares
with many others, which is to glorify the mythological solidarity of
earlier or more primitive times. Revelations are in store for him, to
take one example, if he turns his historically untutored mind to the
so-called medieval synthesis. Pick a century—the eighth, the tenth,
the twelfth—put it under a sociological microscope, and you will see
cracks, fissures, schisms, lags, struggles, battles, revolts, troubles—in
short, divisiveness everywhere. We look back upon the Middle Ages
and think of retrenchment, decentralization, contraction, and all their
concomitants. We should not forget the walled city, greatly shrunken
after Rome lost its imperial grip, and the fortified monastery, under
sporadic siege from a host of enemies. Internecine warfare, fueled
by tension between kings and lesser lords, territorial disputes, church-

men vying with noblemen, the crown and the cross at odds, Christendom cleansing itself of witches, heretics, Jews, and other unassimilable elements: would it not be a grotesque misrepresentation of the feudal order to ignore this turbulent underside? The twentieth-century Dutch historian Johan Huizinga wrote with unforgettable incisiveness about the waning of the Middle Ages, about the violence and brutality attendant upon a massive society in dissolution. The contrast between that advanced stage and the thousand years that preceded it is, however, only one of degree. Internal stress never disappeared, but it was doubtless exceeded by external threat. Throughout the feudal era, Christendom was encircled and beleaguered. Trade routes to the north and south, previously secure, were lost and won again. Control of the Mediterranean changed hands. At one vulnerable point or another, military invasion, conquest, and occupation by foreign armies took place without surcease. If, as historians from Eward Gibbon to Marc Bloch have contended, feudal society was forged in the fiery crucible of Germanic invasion, then, by the tenth century it was more than half overrun by other marauders. Havoc wrought by fire and sword laid waste a large part of feudal Europe. Brief truces, relative calms before ferocious storms, punctuated medieval history. Bloch's unsurpassed, and sociologically informed masterpiece, *Feudal Society,* begins with "the clang of iron and the clash of shields." We hear the bishops of Rheims, assembled at Trosly, declaring in 909:

> You see before you the wrath of the Lord breaking forth. . . . There is naught but towns emptied of their folk, monasteries razed to the ground or given to the flames, fields desolated. . . . Everywhere the strong oppresseth the weak and men are like fish of the sea that blindly devour each other.[10]

Whence this turmoil? Why such devastation? "Feudalism was born in the midst of an infinitely troubled epoch, and in some measure it was the child of those troubles themselves." But a disorderly environment was also the natural consequence of continuous raids. To civil strife was added the menace of Islam (Arabs or their

---

[10] Marc Bloch, *Feudal Society* (Chicago: The Universtity of Chicago Press, 1964), p. 3.

Arabized subjects), bellicose Hungarians from the East and in force, as well as Northmen, Scandinavians, Vikings traveling in, and disembarking to fight from, their very seaworthy battleships. Gaul, Spain, Byzantium, Italy, Britain—all were under costly and sanguinary siege. Brigandage on land and sea; long and profitable forays with armed "hordes" descending on the plains and ports of western Europe; pillaging, burning, gathering booty; one pagan incursion after another: this is the *mise en scène* against which we must read the feudal saga of Western civilization.

The danger, damage, and destruction from without were unquestionably sizable. Bloch guesses that they induced a state of mind bordering on perpetual terror. Towns were in ruins, some extinguished for good, others to flourish again but with countless scars. Two major Carolingian ports, Duurstede on the Rhine delta and Quentovic, "sank once and for all to the status, respectively, of a modest hamlet and a fishing village." Existing records indicate that bandits caused cultivated land to suffer disastrously, often reducing it to desert. Peasants, driven to despair, for instance in the Moselle, banded together under oath in a hapless attempt to repel the marauders. "Their ill-organized forces were invariably massacred." Walls, palisades, ramparts bespoke a terrible anguish. Peasants groaned, lords were impoverished; and with so much of the countryside unfit for farming, starvation lurked in well-defended towns. Under these blows, the intellectual life that was synonymous with monasticism fell into decay. Havoc extended from the material to the mental realm.

Feudal Europe survived, and by historical reckoning, for an impressively long time. It was not supine. Pagans became Christians and were no less bloodthirsty after their conversion. Reflecting on the gravestones of Scandinavia, burial mounds that to this day display their engraved runes, Bloch notes that they are different from Greek and Roman tombs which, in the main, commemorate the dead who died natural deaths, peacefully, by their native hearths. Those in Scandinavia almost exclusively recall battles and the noble warriors who fought them. Bloch ruminates:

> This attitude of mind may seem incompatible with the teaching of Christ. But, as we shall often have occasion to observe in the following pages, among the peoples of the West during the feudal era

there was apparently no difficulty in reconciling ardent faith in the Christian mysteries with a taste for violence and plunder, nay even with the most conscious glorification of war.[11]

Nor was this reconciliation peculiar to Scandinavians. They themselves had been Christianized in ways their warriors and missionaries were later to apply. Even before such immensely important adventures as the Crusades, Bloch points out that, "To work for the extinction of paganism seemed to the Carolingians at once a duty inherent in the vocation of Christian princes and the surest way of extending their own hegemony over a world destined to be united in one faith. And the same was true of the great German emperors, the heirs of their tradition: once Germania proper had been converted, their attention naturally turned to the Germans of the North." Missionaries went forth preaching the gospel to Danes and Swedes. "As Gregory the Great had once contemplated doing with English children, young Scandinavians were bought in the slave markets to be prepared for the priesthood and the apostolate." [12]

We are the heirs of the heirs of those who created Western civilization a millennium ago. What they made looks more and more unitary as it recedes in time. Temporal, spatial, and societal distance lends itself to this impression. We imagine that in the past a golden air of harmony, cohesion, and happiness suffused our ancestors' lives. Frequently the Middle Ages are held up as a case in point. With the help of carefully studied comparative history, it is part of our thankless sociological task to explode this myth. No society is a seamless web. Every society is in motion. At the same time, none survives in utter chaos. Societies rise, falter, fall, revive, collapse, and form anew. Barring race suicide, man in all his marvelous multifariousness and quintessential sameness, his freedom and his unfreedom, his submission and his rebellion, with continuity running through the discontinuity he cannot avoid—this species as Homo sapiens and Homo duplex can be expected to survive.

[11] Ibid., p. 35.
[12] Ibid., p. 32.

For Further Consideration

1. What are the major types of contradictions that seem to govern the operation of society? Explain each.

2. Why is it appropriate to say that "every society is a living lie"?

3. In what way is sociology a debunking science?

4. Is conflict central to or deviant from the overall norms of society? Explain in terms of:

    a. the Trobriand Islanders.

    b. feudal Europe.

Biological and Cultural Bases

W<small>E ARE</small> accustomed in the social sciences to speak of culture as everything made by man. After Homo sapiens, the mammalian biped, left its herbivorous ancestors to their arboreal existence, an emergent species adapted to a new physical environment by recreating it. Through several protohuman variations represented by the likes of Sinanthropus pikinensis and Gigantopithecus blacki, numerous anatomical changes occurred that shaped the postgraduate ape each of us is today. No one has as yet successfully reconstructed all the phases of organic evolution that led to man and his peculiar cultural or "superorganic" life. As fossil remains and carbon tests reveal more and more about our simian forebears—still missing the link or links that may yet be located—ethnologists, paleontologists, and physical anthropologists present a picture of the interaction between man and nonman more exciting and complicated than any modern science has previously entertained.

Dennis Wrong speaks as a sociologist for an increasing number of his colleagues when he emphasizes the adaptive advantages of man's social skills in developing bodily structures that selectively

4
Socialization

supported those skills.[1] Few persons in this century, except for those educated in the public schools of Tennessee, have doubted that organic evolution made man's social and cultural history possible. That this history had profound effects on our biological nature is more newsworthy. Wrong persuasively summarizes evidence adduced by human biologists like Charles F. Hockett, Robert Aseger, and Ashley Montagu:

> Upright posture, bipedalism, the development of the hand as a grasping organ, the specialization of the jaws and the vocal cords for speech, a more complex brain, nonseasonal sexuality, greater infantile helplessness—all these organic traits that define man as a separate species can no longer be regarded simply as a precondition for culture and human social life, but they are themselves products of a process of natural selection that favored increasing reliance on culture. Upright posture, a foot adapted to running, and a large brain capable of storing information aided man's survival in adaptation to a new hunting way of life on the African savannahs. The reduction in the size of his teeth and the recession of his jaws became possible because many of their functions were taken over by tool using and tool making. These are but a few examples of physical traits which have undergone evolutionary change in response to cultural pressures.[2]

We are finally able to infer that man not only reacted to "nature" but acted on it and on himself through the cultural alteration of his own biological makeup.

Behold the featherless biped with opposable thumbs, a large cortex, a complex nervous system: this strange organism blessed and cursed with consciousness. Under the aspect of eternity—or for as long as one supposes the earth has been habitable—he is a latecomer. Culture, our greatest creation, supplied man in all his multifariousness with a survival kit roomy enough to contain the instruments of self-destruction. In the long run, entropy, a general running down of the universe, a further cooling of the sun, an ultimate Ice Age could do us in. In the short run, in the mathematically calculable future,

---

[1] Dennis H. Wrong and Harry L. Gracey, eds., *Readings in Introductory Sociology* (New York: Macmillan, 1967), pp. 12–16.

[2] Ibid., pp. 12–13.

mankind makes or breaks itself. That process, whether it results in cultural transcendence or race suicide, would be wholly in keeping with the human drama that has unfolded up to this point. The species is genetically, psychologically, and culturally equipped to prevail, at least for a while—or to go down and out, and by no other hand than its own.

Man the animal and man the human being merge. Each with a cluster of positive and negative qualities helps to produce a situation as mutable as it is immutable. The newborn infant, the neonate, cannot escape prolonged parasitic dependency. Without adult protection death would surely ensue. Pulling, sucking, grasping, wriggling, the infant organism cannot fend for itself. At birth, the eyes do not focus properly so that objects in the external world (which is not yet structured as such) are undifferentiated; it is not possible to turn over or sit up because the backbone has yet to be completed through myelination, which, with luck, will soon take place. In short, we are born helpless and remain so, or very nearly so, throughout our earliest years. The weak and dependent infant is "aware" of only his inner tensions and biological needs, but not of what they are, much less how to allay or gratify them. Yet, very shortly, to join others as a member of his society, he will have to master a complex range of techniques, beliefs, and values. When this happens, we say of him that he is socialized.

The baby, the human (or more accurately, prehuman) infant, has unfocused biological needs, while in the lower orders of animal life behavior is governed by predetermined mechanisms. In these orders learning is of minimal importance, although it takes place even among insects. But experience does not accumulate nor is behavior basically modified without previous biological changes. The environment man builds for himself is qualitatively exclusive to his own species. Only man adds, stores, and transmits a great deal of what he learns. Every baby starts from scratch, something mankind never has to do. Thus to date, no major invention, the wheel, the compass, the plow, the forge, the dynamo, has had to be rediscovered. Specific peoples now and then suffer technological devolution. So far mankind does not. The human toolbox grows as its contents multiply. Besides the rules man has made, his tools are available to each new generation. They are fractionally absorbed and marginally modified at uneven rates and in various guises by those who perpetuate culture.

The Role of Communication

At first the baby appears to be an unlikely candidate for the future performance of so awesome a function. Subject to internal pressures, hungers, tensions, and drives, he is totally lacking in means to ease or assuage them. He does not know what object or what action will relieve his discomfort. People who have already been socialized know or they know how to find out; they alone can reduce the tension. When an infant cries, he may be hungry, wet, cold, stuck with a pin, or simply in need of being held. His mother, in tending to his needs, communicates to him the cause of his discomfort. Only then, on an additive and repetitive basis, does he learn what was wrong. Since biogenic infantile needs can only be satisfied by a mother, or someone acting in *loco parentis,* they soon and insensibly blend with sociogenic needs. Even in the first few weeks of life, interstimulating and meaningful contact must occur with some frequency. Perceptions, discriminations, and actions center upon persons instrumental in satisfying needs related to sustenance, sleep, elimination, and other physiological functions. In early infancy the child, by crying, establishes an elementary sort of social relationship, and by his mother's response he learns the meaning of his action. Even in its meagerest beginnings, socialization and enculturation depend on the communication of meaning and value. Only as he is able to assimilate the many meanings of social action and the value placed upon them does a child enter and participate in that fragment of world culture that will eventually be his.[3]

As he repeats the process of communication by crying—and even crying has infantile nuances—the child gradually acquires a repertoire of other gestures. Trial and error teach him which responses to

---

[3] I have drawn here and in other parts of this chapter from Joseph Bensman and Bernard Rosenberg, *Mass, Class, and Bureaucracy: The Evolution of Contemporary Society* (Englewood Cliffs, N.J.: Prentice-Hall, 1963). See especially Chapter 2. The views expressed therein are drastically revised.

expect. He communicates a range of emotion, from pleasure to rage, more effectively than before. He also observes that different persons respond to his gestures in different ways. Perhaps his mother tends to his pressing needs, while his father merely plays with him and strangers scarcely respond at all. Sensing this differential response, the growing child chooses his gestures and applies them more or less appropriately. Thus, in this hypothetical setting, when distressed, he signals his mother; with his father he is playful; and when in the presence of a stranger, he simply stares, unaware of what to do next. Certain expectations become familiar. Others are unknown, unstructured, undefined. Some will remain ambiguous, amorphous, vague, and variegated to the point where they can be counted on to produce intense adult anxiety.

The Communication of Roles

A socially defined or collective expectation is called a role. It consists of the probable reaction that will be evoked in an individual by others under specified conditions. Without the roles assigned to us by our culture, group life founded on interpretative interaction among human beings would be impossible. Role expectancy calls forth role fulfillment often enough to supply the glue without which society would come unstuck. It is nevertheless so precariously constructed that the thoughtful sociologist finds himself haunted even today by a fundamental question, which in one way or another all his predecessors (including the social philosophers of ancient Greece) have raised, namely: "How is society possible?" With role theory we are able to offer a provisional, partial, and paradoxical answer, but only in the never-never land of a utopia—far outside any space-time continuum that has yet encompassed us— can we deem that answer to be definitive. Role expectancy points to conduct suitable for a specific status. Status refers to the individual's position within a social order. And that position is determined by the existing division of labor. Given an inconstant division of labor and shifting positions within it, status and role are surrounded by uncertainty. Their limited efficacy should cause the student of social phenomena less wonder than that they work at all.

With that cautionary word, and a promise to enlarge upon it in subsequent chapters, let us return to the inexhaustible business of socialization. We left the parent acting as sole cultural agent, conveying to his child, through gestures of approval and disapproval, what is expected of him. Role-playing, however, takes place on something more than the interpersonal level that meets the eye. Whereas the infant recognizes only his physical discomforts and tensions, parents come to their relationship with children bearing a great many cultural expectations and definitions of behavior. They therefore judge the child by applying standards, values, conventions, and customs that have become second nature to them. It is in keeping with parental norms derived from a large culture complex that demands are made on the child. Only in the earliest stages of infancy are the child's demands paramount. Thereafter, as the child matures, he discovers that some of his demands are met and others are not. His parents begin to say "No!" and to make it clear that only certain forms of behavior will evoke the response he seeks. An increasing multiplicity of do's and don't's descends upon him. He more or less yields to the barrage. We cannot quarrel with two eminent students of human personality, Clyde Kluckhohn and Henry A. Murray, when they attest that: "After countless protestations and rebellions, the average child, with great reluctance, learns to do these things (even those that are 'repugnant to his feelings'), to the extent of conforming to most of the patterns which are considered normal for his age." [4] One drawback in this formulation is its implicit and lopsided behaviorism. Like most learning theorists, Kluckhohn and Murray uncritically accept the Law of Effect, which states that children or others undergoing socialization are totally responsive to rewards and punishments. The infinitely pliable young do those things for which adults reward them and abstain from those for which adults punish them. If so, what do we make of the "countless protestations and rebellions" that outlast infancy and

---

[4] Clyde Kluckhohn and Henry A. Murray, *Personality in Nature: Society and Culture* (New York: Alfred A. Knopf, 1948), p. 23.

childhood? Who is "the average" child? What patterns are considered "normal" for his age? There is more here than Pavlov's canine subjects ever salivated on. *Parents "learn", too,*

Identification

Social learning used to be characterized as imitation. Then the psychoanalysts added identification. Each carries us—once again, too smoothly—toward greater enlightenment. We are reminded that although parent and child communicate, it is the parent who responds to the child long before the child responds to the parent. In his earliest exchanges, the child appears to be all-powerful: his little repertoire of noises quickly, effectively, and so to speak, magically, produces the desired results. With greater maturity, however, he realizes that he is not omnipotent, that on the contrary, his parents have the power to do much that is far beyond his capacity not just for themselves but also for him. Gratification of the child's wants depends on his parents. Seeing this situation, the child wishes to be like his parents, to share the adults' apparently unlimited powers, and to receive the benefits of affection and approval from those prepotent figures. The illusion of omnipotence remains; only its locus is altered.

The child adopts attitudes and other norms from his parents in order to become like them. He imitates, and in his own childish way, mirrors their speech, gesticulations, and general comportment. He begins simultaneously to enact the roles of parent and child. He, for example, gives orders to himself and carries them out (with resultant confusion, slowly eliminated, in the use of personal pronouns). These attitudes and behavior patterns are presumably no longer altogether external; having become part of his personality, they are more than mere constraints to which he must bow. He is said to have absorbed parental values, to have internalized, interiorized, or introjected them, and to have done so in order to be more like those persons in his environment who are already socialized. If his character has a backbone—which is highly problematic as I shall presently suggest—it will perhaps tend to be formed a bit more by this normative experience than by others. Through identification, then, much of the parents' culture is selectively, but not altogether predictably or securely incorporated in the child; and he is on his way to active reciprocal membership in his society.

The Emergence of the Self

Role-playing is instrumental not only in socializing the child but also in the emergence of the self; the child develops a growing sense of identity and individuality. There is no self-consciousness without consciousness of others, and neither emerges spontaneously. A sense of separateness from others comes only with a sense of relatedness to them. The seeds of likeness and difference are planted at once as we associate with people from whom we are torn apart even as they enclose us.

When the child learns to speak or otherwise to symbolize, he is no longer imprisoned in infantile autism or egocentricity, with its limited but absolute perceptions, and then a decisive transformation —nothing less than humanization—begins to take place. The child speaks, and hears himself, as if he were hearing someone else. He notices that others respond to him and at the same time that he can respond to himself. Gradually he is able to conceive, to "imagine," in advance the probable response his speech will elicit in others and therefore to accept or reject the expectancy he arouses in them. The memory of repeated responses to his use of language enables him to think of, that is, to anticipate, even in their absence, how others will react to his verbal cues. Moreover, he is able to censor his own thoughts and actions and attune them to the responses he has evoked in those who are most meaningful to him, his "significant others."

Apart from the mechanical behaviorists, George Herbert Mead, who thought of himself as a social behaviorist (a label now both obsolete and misleading) along with Jean Piaget and Sigmund Freud, was the principal architect of socialization theory. Where Piaget descried a movement from an original state of heteronomy or dependency (on God and godlike parents) to eventual autonomy among peers, Mead differentiated between the "I" and the "Me." For Mead, the "I" suggested spontaneous biological drives and unconventionalized motives that might actuate an individual at any moment. The imagined effect of an action on others Mead designated as the "Me," which corresponds to Charles Horton Cooley's "looking-glass self." Most of us are most of the time Me's, else we could not relate to each other as human beings. The Me is the individual seen as an object to the I.

The Spontaneity of the "I"

The I's and Me's taken together constitute the self, the individual sitting in judgment of his own impulse to act. All of us are sometimes, and always to some extent, I's. Otherwise we would be indistinguishable from one another. The norms round about him that a human being absorbs Mead personified as the "Generalized Other."

The nomenclature is dramaturgic on purpose. It spotlights a fundamental fact about man in society, namely, that he is a wearer of masks, a person in the original acceptation of that word. After awhile, if all goes well, he acts imaginatively before an audience consisting solely of himself, selecting and screening what he will do in advance of his doing it. All does not go perfectly well for anyone. "Perfectly well" for traditionalists and systems theorists ignores or denies the I by making men 100 percent Me's—who if they were that would do nothing but duplicate their own society generation after generation. While stasis is conceptually possible, it has all the human reality of such imaginary creatures as centaurs or nymphs. Neither, on the other hand, are we anarchic I's, going our own way completely insensitive to demands made upon us. Up to a point men are coercible, some more, some less so.

Under the chapter heading "Dissent and Rebellion in the Laboratory," Charles Hampden-Turner recently reviewed several psychological experiments by Solomon Asch, Richard Crutchfield, and Stanley Milgrim. These experiments show how suggestible and manipulable a majority of self-selected undergraduate subjects can be. In a psychological laboratory with prestigious professors and hired stooges to egg them on, they needlessly accede to authority, commit acts of gratuitous cruelty, and so derange their senses as to accept perceptual monstrosities. And a minority, scarcely noticed, although conscientiously reported by each of the investigators, reject the assaults made on their sanity and their humanity. They resist the experimental pressure to cheat, torture, conform, and obey. These are the lone dissenters, the radicals who stop short of nihilism by accepting rational elements in an otherwise deliberately fabricated surrealist nightmare. They decline to join the rigged chorus of voices loudly proclaiming that short is long or that small objects are large and "they argue, often angrily with the experimenter before thrusting their payment back in his face and demanding the learner's release." [5] The Milgrim experiment calls for administration of increasingly painful shocks by a "trainer," who does not know that the whole performance is simulated, to a "learner" who does. The learner is a confederate of the experimenter. He is strapped into a phony electric chair which the trainer assumes to be real; uncharged electrodes are attached to his head, and the trainer is instructed to administer escalating shocks as the victim pretends to writhe and scream in an access of agony. The volunteer receives $4.50 for his services. He is completely misinformed about the experiment, believing its purpose to be a study of how punishment relates to memory and learning. Milgrim really set out to measure degrees of obedience to the command to torture a third party. He was dismayed at the results. From 315 volts to 450, the learner shrieks and struggles with every shock. Levers are elaborately marked "Strong Shock," "Intense Shock," "Danger! Severe Shock." A panel of phychiatrists had predicted that no more than 4 percent would go above 300 volts. Instead, 78 percent did so. They predicted only one-tenth of 1 percent would go to 450 volts and 65 percent did so. "Nearly 30 percent would continue to torture their victim to the end while grappling with him and *holding his squirming hand down upon the shock plate,* while he screamed about a weak heart!" [6]

"The mores make anything right" was William Graham Sumner's

[5] Charles Hampden-Turner, *Radical Man* (Cambridge, Mass.: Schenkman, 1970), p. 102.
[6] Ibid., p. 99.

dictum. To which we add, "Yes, but not for everybody, and not for anybody all the time." The "radicals" told Milgrim, "There is no money in the world that will make me hurt another individual. Here, take your check. . . . This is one hell of an experiment." Some would have no part of it. Many would go just so far and no farther. Hampden-Turner and Milgrim concur in their belief that civilization depends upon just such rebellious people. Both quote Harold Laski to this effect:

> Civilization means, above all, the unwillingness to inflict unnecessary pain. . . . Those of us who needlessly accept the commands of authority cannot yet claim to be civilized men.
>
> Our business, if we desire to live a life not utterly devoid of meaning and significance, is to accept nothing which contradicts our basic experience merely because it comes to us from tradition or convention or authority. It may well be that we are wrong; but our self-expression is thwarted at the root unless the certainties we are asked to accept coincide with the certainties we experience. That is why the condition of freedom in any state is always a widespread and consistent skepticism of the canons on which power insists.[7]

Because reaction follows action, because resistance follows repression or oppression, Laski's condition is ubiquitous. Men do hug their chains—when they are not busy breaking or dissolving them. Projected onto either the narrowest or broadest social scene, this means a circle of friends, a married couple, a tribe, a nation, or the whole of human culture is no sooner settled than it is unsettled. Fission and fusion are the universal components of socialization. Each is absolutely necessary to human fulfillment. The gross distortion of either one can be deadly.

Pathologies in Socialization

Certain pathologies that attend the derangement of socialization are visible wherever we look. They take two extreme forms whose uttermost boundaries are schizophrenogenic. These are isolation and immersion. The obverse side of feeling quite alone, cut off, and really

[7] Ibid., p. 106.

unable to reach others is envelopment: swallowing or being swallowed, loss of self in others, or incorporation of others in oneself. Fluctuation between these extremes or fixation on one of them leads to psychic disorder and social malaise. "Withdrawal-and-return," Arnold Toynbee's famous formula for creative living, fails completely whenever "withdrawal" signifies isolation and "return," immersion. Either way lies a kind of burial; the self is submerged in nothingness, and "hangups" ensue. This is what young bohemians who opt out of our society think that middle-class suburban society has done to them.

"Ontological insecurity" is the term R. D. Laing, a British psychiatrist, has coined to depict the disturbed state he has observed among his patients.[8] Numerous studies indicate that at this moment ontological insecurity typically afflicts the most intelligent, sensitive, and privileged American youth who feel that they must struggle with special assiduity to experience themselves as autonomous human beings. Their quest for ontological security, for being both at one with and separate from the world, must fail if their very being depends on the other *or* on avoidance of the other. Society becomes a directionless void in which "everything goes" because nothing is real. Ontological insecurity in the ruinous existential cycle analyzed by Laing is one of many hazards stemming from defective socialization. Although the hazards are inescapable, their consequences are often reversible. Furthermore, out of the same inherently imperfect process that sometimes eventuates in dementia, there may be found the sociological source of creativity, self-actualization, love, and whatever else makes life bearable to human beings.

Freud, as we all know, stressed biological drives from first to last; for him they were the taproot of human activity. All drives are for Freud basically sexual or libidinal. No matter what their origin, these drives are blind: they represent vague strivings without specific aims or objectives. Above all, they are unconscious, belonging to a sector of the psyche called the id, where repressed energies and memories are also stored. The id is activated by the pleasure principle, which requires complete and immediate satisfaction of biological

[8] R. D. Laing, *The Divided Self* (Chicago: Quadrangle Books, 1960), passim.

demands. Freud was convinced that without socialization the pleasure principle would be given full rein and we could not then hope to be more than rapacious, violent, amoral animals. In Freudian theory, socialization is a product of repression; the id's "biological selfishness" is curbed; and libidinal energy moves toward socially acceptable channels. Repression is the price man pays for civilization. (He pays by incubating neurosis and psychosis in infancy.) Repression is accomplished through identification with parents or parent surrogates who disallow antisocial and anticultural drives.

Human personality, formed in this crucible, is triadically divided by Freud into the id, the ego, and the superego. The ego is the conscious component of personality. While restraining and checking the id, the ego defines opportunities and goals, as well as "reality." It operates on the reality principle, subduing the pleasure principle, testing reality, making exploratory motions to determine what effect they will have. The reality principle implies a painfully acquired capacity to forego immediate gratification in the interest of long-range objectives. One postpones pleasure now to achieve something else at a later date. In the infant who has no ego and who cannot help being overwhelmed by needs that cry out for satisfaction, no such postponement is possible. Some people remain at this infantile level—into which some others, once socialized, then asocialized— tend to relapse. Most outgrow it. The superego is created mainly by internalization or introjection of parental authority, and embodies the principal norms of any given society as they are taught to the young. The superego keeps the ego from indiscriminate pleasure-seeking as it directs libidinal energy toward culturally acceptable goals.

Viewed psychoanalytically, the pathologies of socialization are infinite. Elsewhere, Joseph Bensman and I have dealt with several of these. See footnote 3 on p. 67. Let us review a few.

Since socialization and personality formation are based on repression through identification, the techniques of repression are most important. Theoretically, a child learns to distinguish between the acceptable and the unacceptable by what his mother and father allow or deny him. At the same time, they project their images in making demands on him. If the child goes unrebuked, and remains unaware of limits, identification will be badly inhibited. His biological drives are likely to dominate him while, with an underdeveloped superego, he is unable to defer their gratification. This psychic equipment puts him on a collision course with his society; its custodians are authorized to prevent uninhibited instinctual behavior.

Overrepression is equally serious, leading, as it does, to a denial of urgent biological impulses and a weakening of the ego. A superego overloaded with prohibitions places pressure on the ego to block the insistent id. Plagued by this intrapsychic conflict, a person suffers paralysis of the ego: he may be unable to act at all, retiring to a state of narcissistic isolation, the schizophrenic world he alone inhabits. Even when superego inhibitions are not so potent, an extraordinarily stern superego provokes anxiety and guilt. If successful socialization consisted of a deeply internalized morality centered upon biological repression, few of its survivors would remain this side of the madhouse.

A powerful "puritanical" superego also interferes with recollection of forbidden wishes once entertained and of past antisocial actions. If banished from consciousness, they are technically said to be repressed. They then recede, along with the id, into the unconscious. However, a person's repressed desires and wishes, although they cease to be conscious, are never entirely forgotten; instead they become an additional, if obscure, source of further guilt and anxiety. They may direct the ego in its conscious action even when the roots of this action are known neither to the ego nor to the actor.

Too much repression, a superego swollen with taboos and surrounded by temptations, is calculated to unbalance the individual. When personal neuroses and defense mechanisms are standardized, they clog the channels of communication, becoming a crucial factor in social relationships by attracting similar types of people who coalesce, organize, and work their neuroses into the culture itself. In this sense, it is legitimate to say that a culture, or some significant segment of it, is neurotic. Neuroses can be woven into the fabric of a society. As Freud surveyed his own bourgeois Victorian milieu while serving as psychotherapist to some ladies and gentlemen of Vienna, he learned to heal hysteria and to track it down. Early sexual repression and subsequent amnesia were the villains of this piece. Yet, as Dennis Wrong has reminded us, Freud acknowledged in his masterly "metapsychological" work, *Civilization and Its Discontents*, that many people, perhaps a majority, do not have superegos. Of such people he wrote that they "habitually permit themselves to do any bad deed that procures them something they want, if only they are sure that no authority will discover it or make them suffer for it: their anxiety relates only to the possibility of detection. Present-day society has to take into account *the prevalence of this state of mind.*" [9] (My italics.) Not the overblown superego, the heavy conscience, the weight and terror of guilt but its opposite, a weak or nonexistent superego, the normlessness or deregulation that Émile Durkheim was to baptize *anomie*: this for a profoundly pessimistic Freud was also central in "present-day society." The harsh Hobbesian judgment is consistent with Freud's general theory of socialization.

However anomic or alienated a person may be, he is never totally lacking in a sense of good and evil. That sense even outlasts all capacity to communicate with other human beings; it can animate a psychotic (and in catatonic schizophrenia it can throttle, silence, and paralyze him) despite his isolation from everyone else. Indeed, conceptions of right and wrong, of good and evil, are everpresent in any human population regardless of how fully or superficially its members have been socialized. Consequently, it comes as no great surprise to those of us who have been involved in studies bearing on this topic that these terms should have proved meaningful and productive.

In a recent triple-city study of impoverished youth, Harry Silverstein and this author conducted long informal interviews with a wide variety of ethnically varied, officially delinquent and nondelinquent adolescents. The cities were New York, Chicago, and Washington, D.C., within which we selected the economically most deprived neighborhoods for intensive research. Our in-depth tandem interviews (with two interviewers and one respondent at a time) ranged

[9] Sigmund Freud, *Civilization and Its Discontents* (Garden City, New York: Doubleday Anchor Books, 1930), pp. 78–79.

over a multitude of sociopsychological questions. We concentrated on the good-bad boys and girls in our sample.[10]

A Chicago boy says, "A good person don't do nothin'. A bad person does anything." These are vivid definitions so polarized that, armed with them, he is able to be contemptuous of the former while dissociating himself from the latter. We would expect respondents of any type to deny their wickedness—and they do so less than we would expect. We would also expect them to affirm their virtue—but if so here again we are being too simpleminded. One finds rationalizations before the fact ("techniques of neutralization" as criminologists David Matza and Gresham Sykes have dubbed them) and rationalizations after the fact used to justify disapproved conduct. They are often the same rationalizations that Matza and Sykes find among juvenile delinquents in general. We find them just as often among nondelinquents. No one, not even in Émile Durkheim's community of saints, to which I have alluded in Chapter 1, can consistently bring value and action into absolute harmony. And one man's value is another man's poison; neither has much to do with law-abiding or law-breaking behavior. All young people within society are partially responsive to its controls; only the presocialized and asocialized, for example very small children, mongoloid idiots, and psychotics, are somewhat less so. Juvenile delinquents, like juvenile nondelinquents, are socialized, and one category no more or less so than the other. To say this is not to deny that delinquents break rules that nondelinquents obey. But why they do certain things or refrain from doing them is not always normatively determined.

Crisis in Identity

The pioneer work of Mead, Cooley, Freud, and Durkheim—too narrowly interpreted—has conditioned students of the subject to equate socialization with normative determination. Common ob-

[10] Bernard Rosenberg and Harry Silverstein, *The Varieties of Delinquent Experience* (Waltham, Mass.: Blaisdell, 1969).

servation and honest introspection, bolstered by sociological data, lend no credence to the equation. For it is quite possible to be both socialized and anomic, to be conformist and normless. That this condition obtains on an epidemic scale in the large middle reaches of American society most of us have taken for granted at least since David Riesman wrote *The Lonely Crowd*. By middle-class other-direction Riesman can only have meant a specific state of deregulation such that Americans, as they responded less and less to inner promptings, came, through imitation, to look and act more alike. Widespread conformity is as likely as not to issue from circumstances that foster *socialization into anomie*—with people seeking surface cues to replace the norms they do not internalize. Such conformity, with standard deviation, is observably present in the American middle class. No one should be astounded that it is also readily apparent in the American underclass.

Of late and with good reason, much has been made of the identity crisis facing middle-class Americans. Large numbers of them have been troubled by the question of who they are and what they are. Is there any reason for sociologists to doubt a priori that this anxiety is societywide? Why should one suppose that lower-class persons have been unaffected by the general dislocation and personal deracination of our times—which on this head differ from other times only in degree? On the contrary, if many a middle- and upper-class person cannot locate his "true self" nor any active superego in his multiple self, then how much more likely are people at a lower level to be afflicted in the same way. Such piecemeal evidence as we have indicates that they are. If so, then conscience—that burdensome baggage of prescriptions and proscriptions—is thin and tenuous from top to bottom in a society that has lost the bearings it may never too securely have had. Scratch the system anywhere (as Riesman and, more recently, Kenneth Keniston did with privileged but "alienated" Harvard college students, as some of us did with youth in the slums), and unless we are much mistaken, you will find something like social psychopathy. Given their superior education, members of the middle class can verbalize the problem with greater skill than those who have had to attend slum schools. Given their superior income, they can also receive professional help and psychiatric solace. A psychoanalyst like Allen Wheelis, judging by the vague malaise and diffuse discomfort of his own affluent patients, is able to offer a superb portrait of their trouble in a book appropriately entitled *The Quest for Identity*.[11] Following classical Freudian procedure, he peels off one layer of consciousness after another, only to encounter a great void. It is the same void we have encountered over and over among our economically impoverished subjects. (It is the void suggested by a fabulous raconteur, Oscar Levant, who claims that at a masquerade party he pulled off the mask of his hostess, thereby accidentally decapitating her.)

The externals, the trappings, the phenotypic representations are as various as the colors on a spectrum; and the genotype, anomie itself, transcends them all. Sexual, chronological, socioeconomic, ethnic, racial, and regional differences cannot be airily dismissed. We must reckon with them in attempting to make any sensible analysis or useful prediction of very many important variables. Nobody stretches his person, let alone his personality, over a circumambient culture. Each of us burrows into one or more subcultures, there to be bombarded with special values at variance with those purveyed by other subcultures. Social class is a vital form of such subcultural segmentation. When Max Weber declares that class determines life-chances he is on irrefutable ground. Class also determines life-styles. But class is fluid. The elite circulates in a political revolution; upward or downward mobility has a disorienting effect; membership groups (those to which people literally or objectively, and willy-nilly, belong) and reference groups (those to which people aspire) can be at odds. In our little book, *The Varieties of Delinquent Experience* (see footnote 10), Harry Silverstein and I set out to show that for these and other reasons, the sociologist would be well advised to study cultures of poverty rather than *the* mythological culture of poverty. At a certain level of abstraction, all poor people have much in common; but at a still higher level, all people have much in common; and at a lower level their peculiarities are most striking. Study at every level is useful and revealing. It was the burden of our book that if concern for the poor is directed to allevi-

[11] Allen Wheelis, *The Quest for Identity* (New York: Norton, 1958).

ation of their misery, subcultural differences matter more than similarities. With reference to crime and delinquency, we joined those criminologists who doubt that social and economic class is by itself determinative of antisocial acts.

Socialization and Deviancy

Over thirty years ago Edwin Sutherland, a close student of socialization into law-breaking behavior, tried to dispel the notion that poverty, or traits associated with it, caused crime.[12] He acknowledged that poor and disreputable people commit crimes—while drawing attention to the fact that rich and reputable people also commit crimes. Offenders in the underworld and in the upper world were internally differentiated into groups of safecrackers, fee splitters, pickpockets, confidence men, gamblers, tax-dodgers, racketeers, forgers, and so on. At the same time, Sutherland contended that they were all implicated in differential association and social disorganization. Sutherland's insights have yet to be exhausted even in criminology proper. It is nevertheless possible and desirable to carry them further afield. If we retain his concept of differential association as equivalent to socialization, and modify the ambiguous "social disorganization" into anomie, a great deal can be learned about American society and all its subgroups. With this conceptual scheme we need not slight real and vital differences. Sutherland knew that embezzlement and commercial misrepresentation were not the same as bootlegging and prostitution. Types of crime and delinquency are obviously "class-specific." The unlawful acts of a corporation executive are one thing; shakedowns in the organized underworld are another. Still, a judicious application of the scheme makes it possible to trace a red thread of common processes through the entire system.

Our reports on three groups of equally impoverished but ethnically diversified youth illuminate that thread. While patterns of sexual behavior, of fighting, stealing, and schooling are markedly different for each group, self-evaluation (good or bad boy and girl)

[12] Edwin H. Sutherland, *White Collar Crime* (New York: The Dryden Press, 1949).

presents a predictable sameness of responses. Those who hold to a "culture of poverty" thesis might claim further support for their position in these findings. On the other hand, following Sutherland, we suspect that our data point to something more like a universal than a class phenomenon. To proceed by piling one variable on top of another (adding broken homes, sociopathic traits, educational deficiencies, and so on), using poverty as a base, has so far proved to be sterile in criminological research. Practically everybody violates the criminal law; some poor people do not; quite a few rich people do. Selective sanctions are another matter. Poverty substantially accounts for official punishment, but it is no more criminogenic than wealth. Crime as an American way of life—or as a way of life anywhere and at all times—is systematically embedded in the social fabric.

We have discovered that the terms, good boy and bad boy, no matter what connotations they may have for the public at large, are freighted with meaning for young people. At one extreme we encounter the oversocialized boy or girl who is utterly incapable of making his own independent judgment of good and bad. He unquestioningly accepts the visible and official, the certified and respectable judgments of society. He does this even when negative judgments are passed on *him,* and even when he considers himself innocent of accusations on which those judgments are based. Here is a New York boy who has been consigned to a school for the emotionally disturbed, and who, for that reason alone, defines himself as bad:

Do you think you are a bad boy?
Yeah.
Why?
Because I am going to a 600 school.
And that makes you a bad boy?
I wouldn't be going there if I wasn't a bad boy.
Well, why did they send you there?
They said I was smoking cigarettes. They said I was trying to choke other boys. They said I was throwing firecrackers out the bathroom window. They said I was hitting the teacher.
And were you doing all those things?
I didn't throw firecrackers out the window. I didn't try to choke no

> *guy. I did hit the teacher—after she scratched me in the face . . .*
> *and twisted my arm around. I tried to break away, and then I went*
> *like that, and I hit her in the lip.*

Knowledge of his own conduct, in this case of his own innocence, is eclipsed by an authoritative judgment to the contrary. He reasons: since I have been relegated to a school for bad boys, I *am* a bad boy. Conversely, a favorable self-image may be preserved regardless of actual misbehavior, so long as heteronomous youth is able to avoid a head-on collision with official society. The oversocialized boy, once branded as bad, so brands himself:

> Are you a good boy or a bad boy?
> *Now that I am in trouble, I'm a bad boy.*
> But you say you didn't steal anything.
> *Yeah, but I'm still in trouble.*

The rule of moral expediency is not differentiated by sex. For this reason a New York girl who thinks sexual promiscuity is wrong makes her objection to it on purely pragmatic grounds. She feels that "fooling around with boys" produces too great a loss of face. Once your sexual availability is well known, "Around our neighborhood, they just put you aside," you are disesteemed and your marriage-ability is reduced. Getting pregnant is a real problem, but it is catastrophic if you are not sure which of several boys has caused your plight. Therefore be virtuous. An adolescent unwed mother flatly asserts that, "There is no good girls really," and then, a little later, softens the indictment, for she means, "There isn't any good, *good* girls." Finally she clarifies her view, much as we would and as well as we could: "I mean, you find girls who are obedient, but you will not find girls who are good."

Wrongdoing in the slums we studied is avoided by some young-sters even under intense peer-group pressure, but only, or most effectively, if they are heavily fortified by fright, which is a substi-tute for conscience. In Chicago, a girl who never goes shoplifting herself, admits to having gone along with a friend: "She done it, but I didn't. . . . And she got caught. . . . They called her parents, who weren't home, and then they called the cops. The cops came and got her, but they made me go home. They said I didn't do anything." Why didn't she do anything? "Because I was scared. I just knew I'd get caught."

For most of the adolescents we reached, very little was intrinsically wrong. From their point of view, immorality consists not so much in certain acts but in the discovery of those acts. Evil stems more from detection than commission. Nothing has happened until it is known to have happened by those authorized to make private actions into public scandals. This attitude is precisely the one delineated by Malinowski in describing Trobriand Islanders whose youth went unpunished for the violation of sacred sexual taboos unless they were given publicity—which invited remorseless punishment, whether self-inflicted or not.

There are those in our sample who, although they have committed only very petty offenses, and these but rarely, characterize themselves as "bad" solely because they were apprehended. Being caught signifies for them that henceforth they are assigned, and they accept, their status as delinquents. If we invert the situation, it still holds: career delinquents whose behavior patterns are consistently unlawful, through their involvement in the drug traffic or the numbers racket, who have escaped arrest (sometimes by chance, frequently through protection)—almost always define themselves as "pretty good," "just like everybody else," "not so bad," and the like. For such teen-age children of the ghetto, there is no difference between the social self and the private self. "Which is worse: smoking pot or mugging?" is a question we persistently put to adolescents in East Harlem who, nearly without exception, insist that marijuana is harmless. Our tabulations show that more than half maintained smoking pot is worse than mugging. The reasons given for this response boil down to this, that if you are caught smoking pot, even though you injure no one, the sentence you face is stiffer than that meted out for mugging and inflicting an injury on someone else.

On the Gold Coast and in the slum, on Main Street and Park Avenue, in any hamlet and every metropolis, most of us are governed by the moral calculus of prudence and expediency. We consciously or unconsciously weigh the psychic, economic, social, and political risks of an act against its advantages, deciding only then whether to comply with applicable moral strictures or to defy them. For orderly social life to proceed, it is not necessary that many (or any) of these strictures be deeply internalized. Failure to internalize dominant values, but scrupulously to obey them, facilitates socialization and resocialization. If the first few years have been used to implant a moral vacuum instead of a superego, flexibility, adaptability, and conformity to new social situations can be expected from then on. The world is never at a standstill, and the present breathtaking tempo of change outpaces most others. Those who do not bend will break, and they are the men and women most thoroughly socialized to an ephemeral ethic who find themselves unable to renounce principles they have internalized with the same ease that they adjust to shifts in sartorial or tonsorial fashion.

The above should not be construed as an indictment of "these parlous times," which are probably no better or worse than others. I do wish to indict the socialization theory, or, more fairly, the commonest construction put upon it. Dennis Wrong, in his excellent essay on the oversocialized conception of man, helped turn me and many of my colleagues around on this question.[13] We were too susceptible to the tantalizing but insupportable idea that socialization is normally a two-step process. All available contemporary and historical proof (not much, be it conceded, but what else do we have?) suggests that it is normally a one-step process. The generality of men responds only to exterior constraint and a prudential calculation of its impact, and not to an allegedly internalized code that they in fact never did deeply absorb. These people do not murmur when Christianity supplants paganism, when atheism takes the place of Christianity—or when military dictatorship usurps and destroys democratic government. They are all too well, that is, all too poorly, socialized. Tomorrow's creed will be affirmed with all the vehemence expended on yesterday's creed, in whose face it flies—and forsaken in favor of tomorrow's creed. Rapid transitions of this sort are effected with varying degrees of discomfort. Some ride painlessly with the punches. The minority who have experienced profound internalization of values to which they are committed for life (and cherish more than life) cannot or will not accommodate themselves.

[13] Dennis Wrong, "The Oversocialized Conception of Man in Modern Sociology," *The American Sociological Review,* vol. 26, pp. 184–93.

They too are inclined to calculate the heavy price of defiance and pay it, perhaps with their lives. In a mercurial society, anomie may be conducive to survival. Only the moralist will ask: Survival for what?

For Further Consideration

1. What is the role of communication in the socialization of the child?

2. What is a social role? How is role-playing related to the process of communication?

3. What is the importance of identification in the process of socialization?

4. What are the "I," the "Me," the "self," and the "generalized other"?

5. Do the mores make everything right?

6. What are the major pathologies in socialization?

7. Is repression necessary to growth? Why? Why not?

8. Define:

    a. Ego, id, superego.

    b. Conformity.

    c. Identity.

    d. Technique of neutralization.

    e. Differential socialization.

9. What are the pathologies connected with oversocialization and undersocialization?

F ROM our critique in the previous chapter, it should be obvious that classical socialization theory cannot be unreservedly accepted. Logical and empirical objections to the profound thought of Durkheim, Freud, G. H. Mead, Piaget, and Cooley will not go away. They need to be confronted. And yet, this body of ideas with all its shortcomings is more impressive and usable than many detractors are prepared to admit.

A sociologist like Peter M. Hall, for one, taxes Auguste Comte and Émile Durkheim, as his continuator, with sociologism. Hall charges them with complete omission of the individual, but from line to line he refutes his own thesis. If Comte's work was lacking in "the individual as a unit," and Durkheim's "approach was not dissimilar," why were they obsessed with the fear of "excessive individualism"? [1] Our answer would have to be: for no other reason than that these

[1] Peter M. Hall, "Social Factors Limiting the Development of Human Potentialities," in *Explorations in Human Potentialities,* ed. Herbert A. Otto (Springfield, Ill.: Charles C. Thomas, 1966), pp. 154–73. Much of this chapter is built around contributions to this book.

5

Social Repression and Creativity

gifted Frenchmen, each an individualistic innovator, witnessed the moral and institutional dissolution of their society. They thought, in much less than identical terms, that the wreckage around them could be repaired by a renewed emphasis on social solidarity. In Durkheim's judgment, an increasingly elaborate division of labor fosters self-interest; social control suffers a sever setback; and anomie, including egotistic anomie, signals a general breakdown. Far from excluding the individual, Durkheim worried most about, and concentrated on, the individual who seemed to him to be temporarily detached, uprooted, and disoriented. He saw modern society momentarily pulverized as it moved from "mechanical solidarity" to the new "organic solidarity" based on occupational rather than familial affinity. The same division of labor that engendered "excessive individualism" would lead to further social cohesion. Then the individual could be bound more firmly into the social structure, but not so firmly as to impair his flexibility. Durkheim worked these concepts out in three of four monumental treatises, perhaps most extensively and persuasively in *Suicide*. In that turn-of-the-century book, he isolated three types of self-destruction: egoistic, anomic, and altruistic. Egoistic suicide is triggered by personal unhappiness, anomic suicide by detachment from social control and consequent normlessness, while altruistic suicide is occasioned by too much attachment, an overcommitment, to the norms. From this we can deduce that Durkheim was just as much concerned about oversocialization as he manifestly was about undersocialization.

After disposing too handily of Durkheim, Hall goes on to criticize social psychology for its stress on the individual. Unfortunately he garbles and caricatures Mead, Cooley, and John Dewey, while completely ingnoring Freud and Piaget. Cooley and Mead, because they claimed that man and society were but two sides of the same coin, are accused of going "beyond Durkheim" by describing "the socialization process whereby society becomes internalized instead of standing guard outside of the individual to constrain him," [2] which in fact is a preeminently Durkheimian position. It is Hall's opinion that Durkheim's sociologism made man a prisoner, and that was bad

[2] Ibid., p. 155.

enough; but Mead, with his social psychologism did worse by turning man into a robot programmed for action. Two pages later, Hall is back on the opposite and, I think, right track. It is my track as well as his, and it is also Mead's and Dewey's, as Hall acknowledges in this passage:

> Development and growth require thinking and consciousness which depend on diversity, heterogeneity, conflict, alternatives, challenges and change. John Dewey and Mead long ago pointed out that thought and consciousness spring from ambiguity and blockage where an individual must choose between alternatives and then commit his energy to the realization of the goal.[3]

Just so. Mead realized that we are leashed and unleashed, tied, gagged, bound, and freed by the same group pressure that shapes or misshapes us all. He did not reduce sentient man to the status of a robot. Only very careless readers of Mead will vulgarize his philosophy into mechanistic behaviorism. To do so they must overlook the large voluntaristic component in that philosophy. Mead helped us to apprehend the great coercive power of significant others. These others are agents of an inconstant generalized other. They attempt to inculcate rules of a game that are freely alterable. The child learns rules and roles; in time, he learns how to evade and/or change them with or without impunity. Even from a Meadian standpoint, it is our fate to lead lives filled with doubt and mystery. In any collectivity, Mead tells us, one can fulfill his role by "taking the role of the other," a cognitive, empathic, and imaginative act fraught with difficulties. The "Me" that results from frequent repetition of this act is made of less than solid stuff. What then shall we say of the "I"— that portion of the human personality that is ultimately ungovernable?

Like Mead, Piaget was preoccupied with rules of the game. His experiment with Swiss children playing their ancestral game of marbles has been replicated over and over in many parts of the world. Boys from an early age into adolescence have played some such game for centuries in or around Geneva and Neuchâtel where Piaget, with a team of collaborators, originally conducted his inquiry. He

---

[3] Ibid., p. 157.

interrogated boys of different ages about the rules by which they played. The youngest took their rules to be obligatory, inviolable, even God-given. This phase Piaget dubbed theocratic. Somewhat older boys were similarly rigid but tended to invoke the tradition of their fathers rather than divine law in explaining why they could not tamper with rules that had been handed down to them. In Piaget's scheme, this is the gerontocratic phase. Rules are desacralized or demystified only by the oldest group of boys still playing marbles who have reached a democratic phase of development in which they agree to select and modify traditional rules or make up their own. The first two phases are characterized by heteronomy, the third by autonomy, independence, and peer-induced self-determination.[4]

Just as Freud's id is not absolutely synonymous with Mead's I, so neither is precisely the same as Piaget's autonomy or Durkheim's individualism. Not without some misgivings, I have oversimplified each of these concepts in order to point up a common attribute. We may set all the quiddities aside and note with gratitude that classical socialization theory gives us an important measure of human freedom. By the same token, classical socialization theory, while emphasizing a certain unavoidable imperfection in the processes it clarifies, also casts a bright light on social change. Human intractability, plain cussedness or orneriness, being what it is, every agent of socialization, whether personal or impersonal, whether a parent or a television network, is doomed to partial failure. To some extent, the I, the id, the autonomous individual, will out. To that extent, the individual is free—and things will change. Change has many sources; I would not minimize any of them, but few loom larger than this one; in the very same processes by which men are controlled, they are decontrolled.

The Limits of Socialization

Socialization, which cannot but be faulty, leaves a train of positive and negative consequences. It opens a box filled with good and evil,

[4] Jean Piaget, *The Moral Judgment of the Child* (New York: Free Press, 1960).

one stocked from head to foot with the fortuitous, the unexpected, the fresh, the previously unexperienced, and a collection of unsuspected or untapped resources. These consequences add up to a kind of willpower that kills as easily as it serves. Their combined effect is to reveal man as the decision-making organism that, for better or worse, he must be. Socialization casts every one of us into a mold, but never quite the same mold. We emerge looking, feeling, acting, and reacting much like our neighbors—and sufficiently unlike all of them to be independent entities. Rough edges, quirks, peculiarities, peccadilloes, eccentricities insure a less than perfect fit between man and society. Insofar as it is imperfect, he is his own man, on a leash but free to roam within its boundaries. If and when it dawns on him that despite limits he is a relatively free agent, his liberation will be welcome and exhilarating to some, fearsome and terrifying to most. Part of our paradoxical condition is that we can choose to expand the circumscribed freedom at our disposal or choke it off altogether. The novelist, John Fowles, sums this up as well as any practicing philosopher or social scientist, in two observations:

> We are in fact confined to the courses of action available, perceivable and feasible to us. I cannot choose whether to be a woman or not because I was born male; and so on. Yet there remains the fact that we all have experience of situations when we *feel* (and more importantly, an outside observer can feel) we choose freely. We are perhaps, are almost certainly, machines; but we are machines so complex that they have developed a relative freedom to choose. We are in a prison cell, but it is, or can be made to become, a comparatively spacious one; and inside it we can become relatively free.[5]

Again:

> Chess permits freedom of permutations within a framework of set rules and prescribed movements. Because a chess player cannot move *absolutely* as he likes, either in terms of the rules or in terms of the exigencies of the particular game, has he no freedom to move? The separate game of chess I play with existence has different rules from your and every other game; the only similarity is that each of our separate games always has rules. The gifts, inherited and acquired, that are special to me are the rules of the game; and the situation I am in at any given moment is the situation of the game. My freedom

[5] John Fowles, *The Aristos* (New York: New American Library, 1970).

is the choice of action and the power of enactment I have within the rules and situation of the game.[6]

Fowles's imagery is no mere exercise in poetic license. It is a distillation of the insight toward which many of us are feeling our way as we cross a multitude of disciplines. One point at which those disciplines intersect is in the common exploration of human potentialities. A dip or two into Herbert A. Otto's recent compilation of materials (see footnote 1) on this exciting subject can prove richly rewarding. Afterward, even if the reader continues to agree with Shakespeare's Ophelia, that, "We know what we are, but we know not what we may be," it might also strike him that we would know considerably more about the first if we knew a little more about the second.

Take both ends of the life cycle; look at the young and the old; and bear in mind that so long as we live, socialization is an open book. In Otto's anthology, Rudolph Dreikurs makes several of the most telling points about children.[7] As adults we are amnesiacs. Disconnected bits and pieces, and not much more, come welling up from the first few years of life. Recall, even by free association in extended psychoanalysis, is at best a fishing expedition. The catch is uneven and uncertain from patient to patient, if only because it must be filtered through a powerful censor. Our own childhood remains enigmatic to us. Can the professional historian be of any assistance? With rare and recent exceptions, he has displayed little interest in the very young of any epoch. We have a right to expect more from psychologists, and they do not entirely disappoint us. Freud himself, who believed that the first five years of life were not only formative, but fateful, that they could never really be undone, did not systematically—or unsystematically—observe and record infant care and child development. His daughter Anna, along with Ernst Kris and others, has sought to fill some of the worst gaps. She and Kris established what was supposed to be an annual inventory of published findings called *The Psychoanalytic Study of the Child*. It still appears with some regularity—and I fear, with diminishing

[6] Ibid.
[7] Rudolph Dreikurs, "The Development of the Child's Potential," in *Explorations in Human Potentialities*, ed. Otto, pp. 223–39.

returns. To their credit, Anna Freud, Ernst Kris, and their coworkers have insisted on devising methods for the confirmation or disconfirmation of Freudian hypotheses about infancy. We await the payoff.

With Piaget, we have systematic study. His fascination with children, from the moment he began looking closely at his own offspring, has lasted over a long lifetime. Piaget's direct, sustained, and replicable observation has been enormously instructive. Thanks to it more than to any other single source (and there are by now many other valuable sources) we have more than a glimmering of knowledge about the properties, qualities, and abilities of childhood.

Human Potentialities

In his pioneer study of children's games, Piaget was impressed by the complexity of many of the rules that a toddler was able to master. Nothing of comparable complexity is ordinarily conveyed to little children in nursery school, kindergarten, or the early grades of primary school. As Director of the Jean Jacques Rousseau Institute, a teacher-training center in Geneva, Piaget did exert a strong influence on professional educators. If they take his investigations into account, it is harder than ever grossly to underestimate the child's cognitive capacity. Slum children, rated as ineducable by unsympathetic teachers, solve difficult problems and make complicated calculations. The same pupil who is stigmatized as hopelessly stupid in school may perform brilliantly on the streets, shooting craps, playing poker, learning the rules of his game.

Even the infant's incapacity has been exaggerated. Dreikurs offers many concrete correctives, referring to a multitude of validated examples in which infants "size up a situation," succeed in getting adult attention, and respond instantaneously when parents change their tactics. He mentions this interesting case in point: "Normal infants born to deaf parents usually cry without making any sound; they do not waste any effort. Later, when they lose their tempers, they stamp with their feet or cause vibrations when they want to attract attention." [8] An educated guess, that children could within

[8] Ibid., p. 230.

their first ten years acquire all the knowledge now obtained through higher education, sounds much less outlandish than it used to. Few adults suspected a little while ago that newborn infants were capable of swimming. Current research indicates that when cast into water, because of a gag reflex that supposedly disappears at the age of six months, they are prevented from drowning. Dreikurs, perhaps too enthusiastically, believes that this discovery could revolutionize the life and development of children: "One merely has to visualize its effects on the self-concept of a child which he develops in his early experiences." The human infant's helplessness, so pronounced on account of initial immobility, would change as he "became free in his actions and directions, using his limbs and muscles and developing his brain as he is free to decide where to go." [9]

However that may be, inside or outside an aquatic setting, there is little doubt that we could sharply increase the pace of physical and mental growth. (Whether we would want to, whether the side effects would be too costly, is a separate and serious question.) Just as sphincter control is achieved in certain preliterate cultures long before it is thought to be physiologically possible in our society, so children can learn arithmetic far sooner than at the age level we set for them. Instruction of the very young, by visual and tactile experimentation, proves that they learn a tremendous amount through play. Traditional pedagogy will never reach them. A radically new approach could do the trick. If learning becomes playful and pleasurable, as fun replaces drudgery, children will not only have realized an immensely greater potential but they will do so without being deprived of their childhood. Until recently, gifted children suffered for being classified as prodigies. But what if many or most of them can be prodigies? Omar Khayam Moore has conclusively demonstrated that small tots, regardless of formal intelligence quota (IQ), can learn to read. Dreikurs reports that a Jamaican music teacher has taught all of her very young charges how to compose music of some quality and complexity, such as fugues and sonatas. Also:

> The Japanese Susuki is teaching unselected groups of children, ages three to five, to play the violin, with startling results which are

[9] Ibid., p. 234.

> noticed by the musical world. It is quite possible that many other skills and abilities . . . can be acquired in this way, such as time perception, orientation in space, a deeper grasp of people and the perception of new patterns of various kinds.[10]

One finds irresistible the inference this author draws after marshaling and reviewing only a fraction of the evidence, that any new ability would increase the child's, and mankind's, mastery of life.

If the young can fulfill themselves more thoroughly than we ever before supposed, what about the old? Is their general state of senescence, decrepitude, infirmity, and uselessness inevitable? To that kind of question, Leonard Pearson, a specialist in aging phenomena, replies:

> While there are many unfounded assumptions about human behavior at all ages, those that prevail about the aged are the most pernicious and the most ubiquitous and will be the most difficult to root out, because most of them have existed since antiquity. In one sense a mass delusion has existed in this country and in other Western cultures regarding the aged, and this misconception is only now beginning to show a break with "unreality." [11]

With that, Pearson sets about exploding selected myths and fallacies in light of much new scientific data.

Intellectual vivacity, memory, and sexual activity need not decline in old age. The alleged male climacteric, for instance, seems to be less of a biological fact than a cultural artifact. Indeed, J. Gebhard, director of the Kinsey Institute of Indiana, is convinced that declining sexual activity in males is a peculiar product of Western civilization. Modern medical research fails to support the hoary belief that mere passage of time causes specific degenerative diseases. Feebleness, tremulousness, poor gait, and stooped shoulders are evidently not innate stigmata of aging. More and more the prescribed antidote to these symptoms is exercise. And exercise of the whole body includes exercise of the brain cells. Clearly, premature or inappropriate retirement, abandonment, and isolation, all socially prescribed, can interfere not only with productivity but with longevity itself.

[10] Ibid., pp. 237–38.
[11] Leonard Pearson, "Aging Phenomena in the Perspective of Human Potential," in *Explorations of Human Potentialities,* ed. Otto, p. 112.

Pearson cites a recent study of S. J. London that will surprise many readers but no art historians. London pored over the biographies of some three hundred and fifty composers and conductors, going back about a thousand years. Pearson condenses some of the findings:

> A large number of composers lived into their eighties and nineties and were productive throughout most of their entire adult life. What is more surprising, though, about the creative activities of these men is the indomitable spirit which they displayed in overcoming the debilitating effects of physical disease or injury.[12]

Recent examples are those of Arnold Schönberg, Austrian-born American composer, whose heart stopped beating for awhile—six years before it stopped beating altogether. An intracardiac injection revived him the first time, and he kept working until his second and final death, in 1951, at age seventy-seven. Frederick Delius, the English composer who died in 1934, suffered during the last twenty-two years of his life from progressive quadriplegia and blindness, but nevertheless spent those busy years constantly composing even though it meant giving musical dictation to a secretary. Perhaps the most remarkable case was that of Béla Bartók, the Hungarian composer who died in 1945. He was sentenced to a quick death by leukemia in the nineteen forties, but was unexpectedly commissioned by Serge Koussevitzky to compose his first symphony in America and brought it to completion over the next two years. Would it be too much to say that creativity in the arts, in the sciences, and no doubt in all other spheres, is life-giving?

The example of Bartók puts this writer in mind of a case he knew at firsthand, that of the Nobel Laureate, physicist Leo Szilard. Szilard helped compose the letter signed by Albert Einstein and addressed to President Roosevelt during the Second World War, which stated that with the splitting of certain atoms, it might be possible to manufacture an atomic bomb, and that this weapon would be deadlier than any ever before imagined. Two such bombs were manufactured, and Szilard, joined by some of his fellow physicists, petitioned President Truman not to drop them. President Truman

---

[12] Ibid., p. 121.

heeded other advisers. Hiroshima and Nagasaki were devastated; the war drew to a close; but a final thermonuclear apocalyptic vision immediately materialized. Szilard, who had been involved with Ernest Rutherford, a British physicist, in producing the first chain reaction, was appalled at the destructive force he had helped to unleash. He forsook physics for biochemistry and then neglected biochemistry in order to agitate for peace. In 1960, wasted from the ravages of terminal cancer and refusing medication to keep his mind clear, Szilard secured network television time. From what seemed to be his deathbed in New York's Memorial Hospital for Cancer, the enfeebled scientist pleaded for military disarmament and political reason in international affairs. Some months later, Szilard spontaneously recovered from his fatal illness. (Baffled cancer researchers have privately told me of perhaps two dozen authenticated cases of spontaneous remission from terminal cancer where the possibility of misdiagnosis was close to nil.) Soon after his release from the hospital, Szilard took up residence in a Washington hotel because of its proximity to congressmen and other politicians who might be influenced by him. He wrote and published a novel, otherwise devoting his life to practical plans for achieving international amity. For the several remaining years of his life (he died of heart failure in 1964) Szilard was his old plump and bouncy self. A sense of mission, a deep-seated passion for some achievement, not necessarily as grand as Szilard's—which was after all nothing less than the salvation of mankind—may also be life-giving.

To enhance and not simply to prolong human life demands a kind of transcendence and presupposes a degree of plasticity our species has never been able to attain. If it fails to do so soon, spiritual or physical extinction is in the offing. Our survival so far is amazing. The next step, like all previous steps, will be hard, even if it is only a baby step toward transcendence. Sidney M. Jouard, a humanist and a psychologist, writing much like an up-to-date sociologist, helps explain why:

> Every goal, every project a man sets *for himself* and sets about achieving—whether it is making something, getting somewhere or becoming somebody—is a gesture of defiance in the face of forces that make fulfillment of this project improbable. The world has an inertia and

a momentum of its own; so has the body as a natural object. This matrix of simultaneous acting forces or "determiners" will pull, push or mold man's experience and action in the way a current carries a twig, or wind and rain sculpture a rocky outcrop—but only if man *chooses to be an object* in the world.[13]

We experience our passivity as doing the familiar or habitual thing, taking "the line of least resistance" or giving in and resigning to the inevitable. It is a choice to do or be whatever is available at any particular moment, but,

> "just as man can be shaped, pushed, pulled or carried by the thrust of past and present forces, so can he transcend this way and propose goals and projects that would never come into being if he had not chosen to risk actualizing them. Man's intentionality, his decision to do or be something is a force in its own right, a force that exists under the sun as surely as do wind, biological pressures and social norms. If this will or freedom of choice is renounced, repressed or resigned, then behavior will indeed be the resultant of specifiable, natural forces." [14]

And it will be lethal in the pluralistic but global village we all inhabit.

The Healthy Society

In writing about human potentialities and the healthy society, Joseph Bensman and I have been freely redundant.[15] Thus, to us, the healthy society is one that enlarges human potentialities as the sick society blocks them. Even if we posit widely shared Western values, it is not possible to venture far beyond this tautology. Furthermore, the common device by which a concept is explained in terms of its opposite in this case creates more difficulties than it dispels. We cannot simply say, as so many of our nineteenth-century predecessors did, that health is the absence of pathology, for by pathology they meant isolable symptoms located in specific political, religious, or economic

[13] Herbert A. Otto, ed., *Exploration of Human Potentialities*, p. 349.

[14] Ibid., pp. 349–50.

[15] Joseph Bensman and Bernard Rosenberg, "Human Potentialities and the Healthy Society," in *Explorations in Human Potentialities*, ed. Otto, pp. 210–22.

spheres. Such analysis encourages segmentalism, concentration on aspects of society and not on organic interdependence, which is a condition so marked that to tamper with anything is to affect everything. Impeding an holistic structural view of man-in-society, this limited focus also relieves the observer of any need to assess the full implications of his position. From his point of view it is impossible to contemplate the broad outline of a healthy society.

To supply such an outline is of course a task that requires much more than a statement of opposition to existing "evils." The bitter lesson man has had to learn and relearn for ages was never clearer than in our time: that the removal of evils may be followed by greater evils. Therefore, to rehearse social symptomatologies as we perceive them, while necessary and desirable, is an insufficient exercise. Nevertheless, it should be said that, beyond a basic split to be dealt with presently, there is extraordinary agreement about those social evils whose extirpation would presumably lead the way to some sort of *summum bonum.*

Although no such phrases were used or known, "the enlargement of human potentialities" was critically important in classical Greek (which is to say, Athenian) philosophy. The ideal polity, as it comes down to us in literature, is one dominated by education through which individual capacities for civil government, physical prowess, philosophical speculation, the sciences, and the arts are brought to an exquisite bloom. This tradition seeks a balance in the cultivation of all these potentialities. It is an Apollonian end that has a Dionysian counterpart in the stress on intensive development of particular faculties, with heightened sensibility and erotic excitement as the spur. By contrast, we have the Spartan tradition that set as its goal neither balanced nor specialized *individuals,* who were to be submerged in a greatly strengthened, or really omnipotent, polis.

Ancient civilization, with comparable cases East and West, set the stage for a titanic conflict, which has yet to be resolved, over the role of society, the state, or any large collectivity. In many guises and forms this conflict is a permanent feature of Western thought. The liberals who were our immediate intellectual progenitors exalted individualism—as had *their* progenitors in the Renaissance. They were naturally fearful of government, which seemed to them either an instrument of oppression or, at best, a mechanical arrangement which, if properly contained, could allow for fulfillment in other areas of life. Collectivist ideologies, left and right, from Sparta on down to the present, subordinate the individual to the collectivity as they elevate distant societal ends far above those that are proximate and personal. In pursuance of collective ends, the individual has had to be restrained, directed, conditioned, controlled, and subdued.

With the spread of modern technology and other manifestations of applied science, this ideological conflict has taken on global proportions. There is thus no point anymore in discussing the healthy society except as it encompasses all mankind. The many subdivisions into which our species is organized provide so many arenas for much the same battle. Doctrines are pitted against each other, and nearly as often, the same doctrine is so latitudinarian that its own elements are pitted against each other. This is certainly true for what passes as Marxism, which when recast into the mold of Marxist-Leninism—or Marxist-Leninist-Maoism or Marxist-Leninist-Castroism—has become a major world religion. So various are the strands in Marx himself that it is fair to play the game of "Marx versus Marx" or to invoke his own language and speak of Marx's internal contradictions.

The young Marx (the only one the psychoanalyst Erich Fromm and a sizable contingent of cultists would like us to remember) was something of a liberal. He also argued, early and late, that history was teleological. In his youth he expressed the belief that man was moving toward a society in which each of its members would be a creative and autonomous being. By and by he saw in the class system and in government, its constant handmaiden, an insuperable barrier to human development. He viewed the propertied who owned land, capital, and chattel or wage slaves, as a force that prevented the propertyless and exploited classes from becoming fully human, while the exploiters and their minions were transmuted into "monsters." Actually, for Marx, class war boiled down to war between dehumanized "brutes" and dehumanized "monsters."

As young men, Marx and Engels allowed themselves the luxury of a utopian blueprint which they present with less heavy-handedness than usual but with as much invective, in *The German Ideology*. There we learn that once the expropriators have been expropriated, in other words, when private property is abolished, the state, like the division of labor, the family, the church, and all other institutional encumbrances, will disappear. Prehistory will finally end; and as history begins and the whole range of creativity inherent in man comes to flower, a truly healthy society can at last emerge. One need hardly labor the point that Marx's understanding of the past (with its assumption that in a golden and primitive past, the division of labor did not exist) was deficient; nor that it was not much better than his prediction of the future (with its assumption that an imaginary classlessness, primitive communism without invidious distinctions, would soon be restored). So-called Marxist totalitarianism, employing means not wholly alien to the more mature Marx, has in this century generated an abject idolatry of collective values, always, to be sure, in the name of other values forever postponed. No system is more inimical to individual development than that which has been spawned under the auspices of men who call themselves Marxists. (This is not to say that they have succeeded in squelching the individual. Far from it. Totalitarianism is a handy name for organized, tyrannical, and oppressive but unrealized efforts to impose total control on human beings.) As for Marx's theory of personality, it has had useful and positive consequences, although ironically enough, more in non-Communist than in Communist countries.

Certain proponents of that theory strove even more radically than their liberal predecessors to democratize the development of human potentialities. In their eyes, these potentialities had for too long been monopolized by privileged, leisured, and ruling classes. Human development was to become universally accessible; and Marx, along with his more visionary followers, assumed that any class was capable of achieving it. He and Engels thought that whether self-actualization did or did not take place was largely, or wholly, a social question. For them, what we now call personality stemmed directly from the work situation where men were obliged to cooperate; and when not allowed to grow in their work they were certain to be stunted. The humanization of man could occur only as society itself was reconstituted so that all systems of exploitation were ended once for all.

Whenever a people is liberated from mercilessly exploitative practices and begins to produce thousands of cultivated and creative individuals, we see that Marx and Engels, as sociologists of work—if not as agitators and economists—were substantially correct. Besides those hitherto impoverished and brutalized societies that suddenly "take off" into productivity and creativity, there are even today in the most economically advanced countries large strata in which talent, ability, motivation, interest, and possible genius are cruelly obliterated. The fruits of their partial "liberation" are a prime source of wonder to them and to us. We and they had been socialized to expect little or nothing from such people. A bit more still seems amazing.

The creative person remains a deep mystery to us; his total makeup is special and personal and probably unique. Yet under adverse circumstances, even if he is inordinately productive, only a minuscule fraction of his potential can be realized. We know how seriously suffocating society can be, what deformations it makes in character structure. We do not know, however, how a society would function if everyone were allowed to reach and enjoy the full measure of his biological and cultural capacity. We may never know. Almost certainly no one now alive will see such a society. One suspects that it would be a quasi-anarchist order such as that envisaged and foolishly predicted for the day after tomorrow by Marx, that it would require the deepest transformation of man and all his works, and that it would still fall short of paradise.

Nor can anyone know at this moment, with real specificity, what there is about all historical societies that has made it impossible for them to tap much that lies within man. The potential is present everywhere. This is, so to speak, our constant. Our variables are the social sources of development and of retardation. They are all most obviously present in the family, that irreducible unit of social organization within whose confines we are raised or maimed, cherished or crushed. Unconditional love, warmth, affection, intimate care, and attention are literally priceless. Their absence inflicts overwhelming and irremediable damage. Problems a relatively healthy child can surmount are insoluble for those who have been traumatized in impaired and disorganized families. A reasonably salutary family environment enables children to mobilize their energies, to face life and deal with it. By identification with mature adult models, they learn how to use a greater-than-average amount of the enormous psychic energy at their disposal. The strong, confident, and loving adult (admittedly a *rara avis* in our world and, very likely, in anybody else's) makes meaningful identification possible not exclusively because of traits he brings to his offspring, but also because of the restraints he imposes on them. These restraints oblige the child to surrender his purely biological, amorphous, and asocial impulses and redirect them to new and old cultural activities.

This is so if for no other reason (and there are plenty of other reasons), than because socialization operates in large part through restraints. Socialization is necessarily that imperfect process I have been trying to adumbrate all along, the more so in times of vertiginous social change. Jack D. Douglas, a young sociologist, arguing that such social change has become the central fact of our everyday lives, has put the case for United States society in two summary paragraphs:

> In 1820 there were approximately ten million United States citizens, the great majority of them English and Scottish Protestants. There were probably three million Negro slaves. By 1910, only ninety years later, twenty-eight million immigrants had been added to the earlier population. By 1930 another ten million were added. By today there have been over forty-four million immigrants, the great majority of them Catholics. There are now twenty-three million Negroes. Nearly forty percent of the population is non-Protestant, with many more percentiles uncommitted.
>
> At roughly the same time that this great tide of immigration was occurring, the United States was being transformed in almost every other way as well. It went from extremely rural and agricultural to extremely urban and industrial, from poor to rich, from one of the weakest to the most powerful, from one of the most isolated and neutral nations to the most internationally involved policeman, from an uneducated, intrinsic society to the world center of education and art, from a society deeply suspicious of science to the devoted leader of the scientific and technological revolution, from a society of individual initiative and free enterprise to one of giant corporations, giant government agencies, graduated income taxes, government controls and long-run planning, from a society of anarchic frontier freedoms to one with vast, complicated, centralized organizations of social control and universal military obligations. In fact, almost all of these

changes in our society have taken place within the last seventy-five years, most within the lifetime of the average adult, and almost all are continuing and accelerating today, while new forms of change are occurring at accelerating rates.[16]

For Western man, it is physically, institutionally, and metaphorically an age of antimatter. Antiutopias and antinovels proliferate; Minimal Art approaches zero; antiheroes abound in literature and in life. As things wind down whilst they wind up at an even greater rate in Asia, Africa, and Latin America, disestablishmentarianism hovers over all human culture. Deregulation, deauthorization, destructuration, detribalization leave our works in an historical rubble heap that rapidly dissolves before our eyes. Amid this wreckage, opportunities for innovation, reinterpretation, selection, and re-creation of culture appear and multiply.

Creativity and Rebellion

Now the child undergoing initial socialization resents and rebels against the very process that is making him human. If the necessary restraint brought to bear upon him is not excessive, he can deliberately reject some of the cultural items presented to him or modify them and experiment with new forms. The selective acceptance, rejection, and reinterpretation of culture may be wholesale or piecemeal, but it is impossible to eliminate. And there, if anywhere, in those choices, lies the major social source of creativity. In what other matrix could sociology locate the genesis of any unique image of the world? When early independence coincides with strong ego development and socially defined media like art and science are at hand, circumstances favorable to substantial self-fulfillment may be said to exist. Norris Fliegel and I have attempted to document this hypothesis, using a sample of men and women, painters and sculptors, drawn from the New York School when New York had over-

[16] "Deviance and Order in a Pluralistic Society," in *Theoretical Sociology,* eds. J. C. McKinney and E. A. Tiryakian (New York: Appleton-Century-Crofts, 1970), pp. 393–94.

night become *the* world art capital and Abstract Expression was at its height.[17]

Circumstances conducive to such an efflorescence, directly experienced within a family setting, are reinforced by the larger society that can reaffirm one's mastery of materials and techniques, can supply them, and can offer as exemplars those who personify past accomplishments and encourage work well done. Contrariwise, society usually presents the developing person with a plethora of restrictions, distractions, alternative rewards, incomprehension, resistance, alarm, and hostility. The genius will be deterred by none of this. Lesser lights fall by the wayside.

It follows (and we owe this formulation to Bensman) that the potentially creative human being must "use" society to extract from it all the support it has to give while mustering his resources to repel available "solutions" manufactured for him as well as attractive or oppressive alternatives to his own natural unfolding. All this implies that one needs to develop in childhood the psychological strength to define his own tasks, to create his own vision and not to let himself be deflected from it. The family can best supply this strength by providing love *and* a sense of limits, but mostly by permitting the conflicts inextricably involved in socialization a certain freedom from overrepression and underrepression.

With all that, it must be added that in contemporary society, the family has only a preliminary and fragmentary role to play. It acts as a primary agency for the entire complex of social relations and institutional patterns that cross our path. Hence it is the total structure of society that eases and facilitates or hinders and prevents "successful" socialization. If the family is seriously defective, if adults are absent by reason of death, desertion, or divorce and neglect or abandonment is the result, human potentialities are snuffed out just as they begin to flicker. If the parents are available but suffer from an incapacitating weakness, extreme brutality, or inordinate frigidity, human potentialities are bound to be diminished beyond repair. By the same token, if a given society so coerces and oppresses parents that they have little to transmit apart from deprivation associated

[17] Bernard Rosenberg and Norris Fliegel, *The Vanguard Artist* (Chicago: Quadrangle Books, 1965).

with poverty, misery, race prejudice, and raw struggle for survival, the loss is immeasurable.

Poverty and Social Repression

Some solution to the intolerable problem of poverty, with its in-human side effects—which may be within our reach, if not our grasp —is a minimal precondition for the release of that vast human potential that has never been touched. For the first time in the United States a national administration, under President Lyndon Johnson, did solemnly commit itself not simply to the patchwork amelioration of poverty but to its extirpation. The revolution of rising expectations that accompanied Mr. Johnson's War on Poverty has, to be sure, been followed by a revolution of declining expectations. Poverty goes substantially unrelieved as the country's strength is sapped in more futile and interminable wars. So far, despite many programs and plans, mere tokens have been proffered to the poor: limited funds are spread over the largest possible number of bodies in the shortest period consistent with inadequate annual budgets. Yet, if the United States stops short of all-out international war (and we are not so short of that fatality right now), any administration will find it difficult to set aside or repudiate ambitious antipoverty programs. With further warfare abroad, we can learn precisely how extensive man's inhuman potentialities are. Otherwise, pork barrel and all, we are in a fair way of releasing many unsung, undetected, and unknown creative capabilities in millions of people.

To overcome poverty and other totally debilitating forms of material deprivation, while a difficult and delicate assignment, is also a rationally attainable one. Other undoubtedly worthy objectives, as yet dimly perceived, are less realizable. What to do, for instance, after everyone's stomach has been filled? For about two-thirds of the world's population grappling with problems of subsistence, such a question seems not only premature but obscene. However, it is the infinitely better-fed superpowers with their deliverable thermonuclear weapons that at present menace our existence as a species. Furthermore, hungry masses in most parts of the world would be much more adequately fed if we could effect a radical reorganization of the international economy. Some experts argue that in half a century—provided we are not all reduced to radioactive dust—economically underdeveloped peoples can be brought above the hunger line. If so, then what?

Then perhaps men elsewhere will have to look to the *quality* of their lives, as those of us who live off the fat of the land have long had the opportunity to do. When this happens, we may all grow more interested in those ideals and visions that radiate out of society—to determine whether we can link them with our personal perceptions. That postmodern or postindustrial society will so provide for us is by no means assured. Monolithic value systems supported by armed force are also possible. They would be guarantors of further instability at a time when civilization itself is most precariously balanced. In a monolithic straitjacket, the individualist (and there is one in each of us) squirms until he is exhausted, finally deriving whatever comfort he can from any elbow room left to him. In due time he can be expected to break out of the straitjacket by striking out blindly, desperately, and promiscuously at "society" as such. The attempt to impose monolithic values, as in the USSR, means sanguinary strife—a nightmare that can be averted only by fostering pluralistic values. A paucity of competitive ideals circulating in society makes it so much harder to combat careerism and professionalism with their commitment to external rewards and disdain for the inner or immanent life. Within the narrow technological perspective, human development signifies no more than the acquisition of specific skills that enable a person to perform his task with appropriate competence no matter what its purpose may be. Then, as instrumental ends are unduly exalted, there is very little of social value to which he or we can tie our private visions.

Here there is a counterforce at work. Again it is the providentially imperfect process of socialization by which a child sees his parents' cynical and fraudulent behavior and, revolted by that sight, is forced to construct values of his own mostly out of those to which an older generation is formally but "hypocritically" devoted. In this manner, youth continuously recreates the half-forgotten ideals of its parents —which is not to say that the well-nigh universal spread of adult cynicism is anything but a formidable obstacle to cooperative or altruistic human development. Youthful zeal, when not literally narcotized by those who turn on and opt out, is too often smothered in a society that handsomely rewards its countless frauds and heavily penalizes those who persist in going their own way. Discouragement, capitulation, and conversion to fraud are probable reactions in a social milieu that stigmatizes anything like the self-imposed discipline requisite for creativity.

Organizational Repression

Marx and his followers were not entirely insensitive to this range of human problems. They were, however, tragically mistaken in their hope that a hypostatized history was about to solve them all. The specter that haunts us well over a hundred years since Marx first loosed his revolutionary bolts is plainly not that of capitalism which, insofar as it exists at all, would be unrecognizable to any nineteenth-century man. And the *soi-disant* Communist revolution (a cover for totalitarian and authoritarian dictatorship) has brought once backward states up to and beyond the levels of bureaucratism and mass manipulation that several non-Communist societies have managed to reach at a slower and less gruesome pace.

Human society, much freer here and much more restricted there, tends everywhere to be overmechanical. By revolution and by evolution, in spite of morally decisive differences in terror, bloodshed, and misery, men make large-scale organizations with bureaucracies to tend and nourish them, as they urbanize and industrialize, adding mass communications to more and more specialization and impersonality. The triumph of technological society brings with it a host of new values, personnel requirements, and skills. It confers a kind of social centrality on administrators, functionaries, and technicians; they then place unbearable pressure on traditional institutions that are so altered as to refashion personality, helping it fit the new regime. To the fore come mechanical efficiency, "interpersonal competence," and disciplined amiability. These are the traits that old-fashioned social critics excoriate as evidence of other-direction and overconformity. The new society has new functions that are considered indispensable. They do not include idle contemplation, the accumulation of useless knowledge, pure science, or any of the impractical arts and crafts. (Be it noted parenthetically that the grim young professional revolutionaries, fueled by fanaticism, are given over to a type of puritannical austerity that, in this respect, is a mirror image of the society they wish to overturn.) There is little room in this order or any that threatens to displace it, by revolutionary or counterrevolutionary means, for the articulation of creative potentialities among men who, while at work or at leisure, must respond to the bureaucratic apparatus that grips them.

Affluence and Repression

To block the individual's substantive interests by artificially narrowing his chosen field, making it all but impossible for him to stretch toward a nonbureaucratic destiny, is dehumanizing. There are other subtler hazards. One involves overacceptance or overidentification. Some college-educated parents who do not enjoy the bureaucratic functions they perform, set out with great determination to support their children's artistic or academic talents—for reasons extraneous to the children but dear to the parents. Parental anxiety, coupled with a desire for middle-class graces, propels numerous youngsters into the half-hearted pursuit of activity which, whatever spark within them set it off, is no longer theirs. Should the spark truly ignite with a serious expression of interest in financially unremunerative forms of self-development, conflict will follow at just that point. Social psychologists like Erik H. Erikson who have pinpointed this danger, tend to view it with less alarm than the passive response to parental wishes and an accompanying loss of any initial drive that may once have been nurtured.

Such are the hazards of good fortune in affluent America. To the extent that they are peculiarly contemporary, most of them are derived from the disenchantment and bureaucratization of society. These are phenomena that have to do with the human spirit, its perils and possibilities. The majority of human beings live even now in a state of semistarvation. We cannot too often remind ourselves of this fact, nor that their redemption from brute existence is a matter of the first importance. And if such redemption is to be achieved by economic development (can poverty be banished any other way?) then we must face up to the continued extension and expansion of bureaucratic structures.

A humanistic sociology might put the problem as follows: How can we chart a course between animal underdevelopment and mechanical overdevelopment? Knowing how deeply beset we are with this normative problem may help men to dream up improvements, concoct experiments, and introduce innovations.

It would be a monumental irony if man's newly liberated potentialities had to be suppressed, perverted, lost, or turned against the self. The human predicament—suffering and death and the consciousness that they exist—is our perpetual lot. The rest is excrescence, which Sisyphus, or Man, may help to erase with his giant boulder as he rolls it uphill once more.

For Further Consideration

1. What are the limits of socialization?
2. How do men transcend socialization?
3. In what way does society block the development of human potentiality? How does society enlarge human potentiality?
4. What are the specific contributions of the family to the development of human potentialities? In what ways can the family block such developments?
5. How do large-scale organizations both foster and inhibit the development of human potentialities?

From the inception of their enterprise sociologists have taken crime into account. Its universality—along with that of religion, the family, and art—could not but interest men who wished to found and sustain a science of human society. The subject was as intrinsically appealing to them as to laymen. At first, however, they did little more than substitute technical jargon and statistical formulae for everyday language. Otherwise their "scientific" conceptions were virtually indistinguishable from those that could at any given time be deemed either official or popular and widespread.

So, for example, sociologists were inclined to treat normal and pathological, conformist and nonconformist, law-breaking and law-abiding social action as separate and distinct phenomena. Worse, these abstractions were frozen into an artificial dichotomy that sacrificed holistic for dualistic thinking. Whenever sociology lapses into what Kurt Lewin, a great social psychologist, has called the Aristotelian or dichotomous mode of thinking, its central vision is lost. By unnaturally opposing and juxtaposing heredity to environment, the individual to the group, or stability to change, we lose

6

Crime and the Man

our way. These sterile dualisms have in fact been invoked to explain yet another false dichotomy: the criminal and the noncriminal. The present generation of sociologically oriented criminologists has moved steadily away from that dead end toward a position others thoughtlessly vacated or gratuitously neglected. More and more of us have sought to recapture the spirit of W. I. Thomas, who began *The Unadjusted Girl,* his luminous monograph of 1923, with these sensible observations:

> It is impossible to understand completely any human being or any single act of his behavior, just as it is impossible to understand completely why a particular wild rose bloomed under a particular hedge at a particular moment. A complete understanding in either case would imply an understanding of all cosmic processes, of their interrelationships and sequences. But it is not harder to comprehend the behavior of the "unadjusted" or "delinquent" person, say the vagabond or the prostitute, than of the normally adjusted person, say the businessman or the housewife.
>
> In either case we realize that certain influences have been at work throughout life and that these are partly inborn, representing the original nature of man, the so-called instincts, and partly the claims, appeals, rewards and punishments of society—the influences of his social environment. But if we attempt to determine why the call of the wild prevails in one case and the call of home, regular work and "duty" in the other, we do not have different problems but aspects of the same general problem. *It is only as we understand behavior as a whole that we can appreciate the failure of certain individuals to conform to certain standards.* (My italics.)[1]

Less than a decade later the versatile scholar Frank Tannenbaum echoed Thomas in characterizing the criminal as a man "like the mass of men, living a certain kind of life with the kind of companions who make that life possible."[2] This note, after having been subdued or extinguished for awhile, is now commonly sounded anew, at least among sociologists. John H. Gagnon and William Simon, students of sexual deviance, are typical in this respect when they take it for granted that, "Deviance . . . may be considered one of the facts of social life. . . ." Or again, that, "There is no form of behavior,

---

[1] *The Unadjusted Girl* (New York: Harper Torchbooks, 1957), pp. 1–2.
[2] *Crime and the Community* (Boston: Ginn and Company, 1938), p. 22.

sexual and non-sexual, that is intrinsically deviant or deviant because of the behavior that it involves." [3]

Such statements are not self-explanatory. We need to study their implications which, when spelled out, correspond to a position shared by most contemporary criminologists of the sociological persuasion. Man the criminal is neither more nor less *man* than Homo Faber, Homo Ludens, or Homo economicus. This is our starting point, our first premise, our basic presupposition. How illuminating the point of view that it suggests actually is remains to be seen. Meanwhile, I now propose to circle around the subject with specific reference to crime in America.

Discussion of crime not only produces heated controversy. It also induces a feeling of omniscience on the part of protagonists and antagonists who think they know all about the "why," the "what," and the "how" of a problem that mystifies more thoughtful people. In the remainder of this chapter, I want particularly to raise doubts, offer complications, and shake certainties—in short, to ask a few sociological questions without which even tentative answers have no meaning. Mindful of that objective, the reader is invited to take off on an initial sortie into the criminological sea of confusion. We will start with the press, drift in and out of scholarship, move around history and politics, and then only attempt to steer a somewhat more rigorous course.

Myth and the Social Definition of Crime

The *New York Times* is rather an austere daily whose editors eschew sensationalism. By and large, its columns are devoid of "news not fit to print." A larger sector of the press specializing in "yellow journalism" feeds, although it evidently cannot satiate, the public taste for prurience, scandal, gossip, murder, mayhem, and brutality. Lurid details of criminal activity, captured in primitive prose and brilliant photography, are deemed to be unsuitable for America's self-styled newspaper of record. They are left to "vulgar" competitors and to other media with more mass appeal.

[3] *Sexual Deviance* (New York: Harper and Row, 1967), p. 8.

On the day these paragraphs are written, however (a Saturday; the edition is thin), our cursory content analysis of the *Times* reveals that considerable lineage has been devoted to crime news. We may begin to grasp our prickly subject by examining two of these items. On page one, section two, where major feature stories appear, the *Times* headline reads: "Chinatown Fighting New Kind of Tong— The Youth Gang." This *is* news. Throw a stone and you will hit someone who "knows" that Oriental-Americans, whether young or old, are the most law-abiding people in this country. If your target happens to be a professional sinologist, an old China hand, he will also probably have explained before 1950 that Mao Tse-tung's Red Army would never succeed in inflicting Communist totalitarianism on China. Although there were notable exceptions, the typical Far Eastern expert felt confident twenty years ago that a collectivist economy and a centralized state were doomed in China. Communists, accordingly, could not succeed. They would never be able to build the full apparatus of police terror into Chinese civilization. Communism, with its obligatory denunciation of reactionary parents by their revolutionary offspring, was un-Chinese. A system so profoundly inimical to people drenched in tradition could only fail. The powerful family structure, which for millennia withstood every other change, would outlast this one too. It did not. The experts grossly miscalculated by extrapolating from a classic culture that had remained flexibly intact for so long that it seemed to be eternal.

A comparable error beset those experts who thought they saw the Chinese way of life effectively transplanted and encapsulated in American Chinatowns where law and order prevailed. Practically every textbook in the field pays its respects to Chinese, Japanese, and Jewish Americans who are said to be the least criminalistic people in our society. They are generally alleged to be, or to have been, so respectful of the law because they are or were so respectful of their parents. The old world tradition in each case taught filial devotion, absolute obedience, total subservience to elders who would one day be transmogrified into revered ancestors. That tradition, in various forms but always with extended kinship control and firm religious commitment, precluded crime. But did it, even in the old world? Not in any old world the sinologist, the Japanese, or the

Jewish historian recognizes. Ancient and modern annals of the Eastern world (or the East European world) are perfectly intelligible to Western readers who recognize the familiar pattern of rape, murder, pillage, incest, adultery, theft, and the rest. The melancholy chronicle of aggressive and dishonest indigenous peoples is monotonously similar in all times and climes. Right at home, from the beginning of recorded history, and even before men codified and transcribed their forbidden or required acts, they regularly practiced transgression of sacred and secular law.

Myths die hard, and no subdiscipline is more bedeviled with them than criminology. The myth of a golden and beatific past, which pervades the Occidental view of Oriental history, also pervades the Occidental view of itself. Daydreams of noble savagery, extended innocence followed by an abrupt and fatal fall, the medieval synthesis, small-town serenity, and agrarian integration all drew their sustenance from that myth.

Tannenbaum, writing more than thirty years ago in a treatise that both reflects and transcends its times, quotes a portion of the 1931 annual report of the New York City Police Department:

> About one half of the Chinese in San Francisco are alleged to be members of tongs. The tongs get their chief income from some form of illegal business, fleecing their own countrymen rather than members of other races. Their members are engaged in or are accessory to traffic in dope, smuggling Chinese into this country, dealing in Chinese slave girls, and gambling. It is said that all Chinese gamblers are tong men, necessarily so from the standpoint of protection. Since the tong is often a blackmailing organization, it is somewhat analogous to the American-Italian black hand, which preys upon wealthy Italians. The Chinese, however, are more helpless than the Italians in a similar situation because American customs and institutions are even more foreign to them, and there is no superior authority to settle their disputes, which cannot be handled without great difficulty in American courts.[4]

Now consider more of the *Times*'s story:

> In recent months, teen-age gangs with such names as Black Eagles and the Flying Dragons have been held to blame for a grenade tossed into one of Chinatown's many gambling parlors, and a street knifing,

[4] Tannenbaum, *op. cit.*, p. 43.

the holdup of patrons of a movie house and a sidewalk machete attack on rivals.

A couple of weeks ago, two radio-car patrolmen broke up an attack in which chains, belts and sticks were used against two Chinese-American brothers and arrested four of the ten assailants. . . .

In the last couple of years there have been repeated reports of youthful gang activities. . . . A Chinatown professional man said: "There are all sorts of gangs, ranging from some real vicious ones to social clubs. Some merchants' groups who sponsored rival tongs in the old days of illegal immigration now have their own teen-age groups who operate from so-called recreation centers.

And so on. Apparently, things have not changed all that much, but their *visibility* has. Groups previously unconcerned about various forms of lawlessness in a more or less self-contained community, now express alarm about them. Officials who once denied or ignored this type of activity—which was neither troublesome nor burdensome to outsiders—suddenly take cognizance of it. Thus do old forms of behavior, scarcely modified for half a century or more, become noteworthy and newsworthy. If troubled awareness persists, with or without significant alteration of that behavior, we have every reason to expect the official Chinese-American delinquency rate to soar. Starting from a point near zero, which was never really close to the mark, an administratively significant but otherwise irrelevant rise of several hundred per cent will be reported. Arrested offenders will materialize who previously were neither arrested nor identified as offenders.

Crime as a Product of Social Protest

Let us inspect a second dispatch from the *New York Times* of June 29, 1968, this one from Washington, D.C. It is headlined: "Poor Defy Police to 'Fill the Jails'" and bears a subhead that reads "Arrested at Capitol after Refusing to Halt Singing." This is part of what follows:

Participants in the Poor People's campaign marched onto Capitol Hill today with the asserted intention of "filling the jails," and the police started to arrest them. . . . A group of 300 predominantly white

Quakers demonstrated in sympathy with the campaign and a group of about thirty joined the Negroes who were waiting to be arrested. The Quakers had been conducting a silent prayer vigil next to a statue of Chief Justice Marshall at the base of the Capitol steps. . . .

Not many men have been arrested, although some have been executed for their refusal to stop singing, but this example is less bizarre than many others that have been fully documented in the literature of criminology. It is a mild manifestation of nonviolent civil disobedience, deliberate and open defiance of laws held to be unjust, unconstitutional, discriminatory, or simply abominable. Its exercise invites penal sanctions. The leader to have perfected this technique was of course Mohandas K. Gandhi who drew his inspiration not only from Hindu holy books but more immediately, from certain writings of Leo Tolstoy and Henry David Thoreau. Brutal exploitation is sometimes more intolerable to altruistic philosophers than to its victims. That the untouchables of India, the serfs of Russia, and the black slaves of America were sorely, if ever so legally oppressed, was more than Gandhi, Tolstoy, and Thoreau could bear. Accordingly, they urged their countrymen to resist "infamy," peacefully pay the institutional consequences, suffer imprisonment if necessary, and so arouse the public conscience as to mobilize it for human betterment. Thoreau, a shy and retiring man but every inch the nineteenth-century Abolitionist fired by John Brown's martyrdom, entered Concord Square and there delivered his world-shaking oration on civil disobedience. When he vehemently objected to his country's participation in the Mexican-American War, Thoreau refused to pay taxes and went willingly to jail for that defection. Thus the famous, if apocryphal, exchange between Ralph Waldo Emerson and Thoreau: Emerson, upon beholding his friend in the jailhouse allegedly exclaimed, "Why, Henry, what are you doing in there?" Came the accusatory reply, "What are *you* doing out there?"—with its clear implication that there are times when all honest men belong behind bars. This attitude is deeply imbedded in one part of the American grain, the part whose twentieth-century legatees have been Eugene Victor Debs, the conscientious objectors of World War I and World War II, the Freedom Riders—Northern zealots going South expressly to violate "illegal laws" of racial segregation and to be incarcerated for so doing—and even more recent cases in point like draft-card burners and other peace protesters. Above them all looms a charismatic figure, that of the Reverend Martin Luther King, Jr., an extraordinary civil rights leader, shot dead like Gandhi, while performing his peaceful and technically unlawful mission. King's followers carry on in King's spirit by Poor People's campaigns and latterly by other devices. Only their total frustration encourages other more violent, if not riotous and insurrectionary, criminal conduct.

Violence as a Product of Social Repression

Another twist of the American grain, on occasion related to the one above, is symbolized by invocations of a higher law, God's law, which rulers are accused of flouting when they make and enforce their own fallible body of law. The Christian martyrs of Rome, like the heretics, sorcerers, Jews, and infidels of medieval Christendom, believed that they were governed by one or another version of that higher law. Flogged, tortured, crucified, flung to the lions, dismembered, decapitated, roasted—true believers went dauntlessly to their Maker. They were sure that perpetual bliss awaited them in the hereafter and as sure that their murderers were doomed to eternal hellfire. Almost without respite throughout much of the sixteenth and seventeenth centuries Europe fought sanguinary international or civil wars in which those who upheld the established faith did battle with those who upheld the not-yet-established faith. Neither side doubted that it stood for the forces of light nor that any enemy defending an imperceptibly different religious doctrine was evil incarnate. The conquest, colonization, and settlement of North America can be understood only against this background.

The higher law prompted religious dissenters, harassed for their criminal beliefs in England, to seek out not only a new England in a new world, but to found a new Jerusalem as well. They joined a little army of adventurers, fortune seekers, ne'er-do-wells, "common criminals," and convicts of the lower orders, men who had been as indifferent to the canonical law as to its secular counterpart

—many of them on their way to becoming bonded and indentured servants. The Church of England split several ways in the motherland. Devotees of each branch were soon congregated in various colonies along the Atlantic Coast. Transplanting their divergent creeds, salting little quiddities with a large dose of fanaticism, they lost no time persecuting one another as vigorously as they themselves had been persecuted. Failing to convert any substantial number of friendly or hostile inhabitants of the land they claimed as their own by force of arms, these colonists began to exterminate the tribal cultures surrounding them. The modern name for their destructive action is genocide, and genocide by any name it certainly was. Today the systematic annihilation of a whole people and all they have created is officially classified as a crime against humanity—at least, in some quarters. Every attempt to institutionalize the law declaring genocide a crime against humanity through even so feeble an instrument as the United Nations has so far failed. To date, the United States, for one, will not sign or formally support such a declaration. Over sixty other nations will.

And yet it was the United States, along with its wartime allies, Great Britain and Soviet Russia, that tried and convicted numerous malefactors, all German and Japanese, for many atrocities, among them crimes against humanity, including genocide. Only at the Nuremberg trials, their sequelae, and at similar proceedings in Japan directly after World War II has the majesty of international law been brought to bear by victorious powers sitting in judgment of the vanquished. The law (except for several Geneva and Hague conventions that bound both sides to certain rules of war that were and are flagrantly disobeyed) did not exist prior to its violation. Technically, it was an ex post facto law of a kind profoundly inimical to Anglo-Saxon legal tradition. That law's constitutionality was nevertheless upheld by a majority of the justices of the United States Supreme Court. For some time this precedent lay dormant, became nebulous, and finally resurfaced pianissimo as an embarrassment. For, while America fought the most unpopular and apparently interminable war in its history, certain draft resisters or draft evaders accused their own government of committing atrocities in Southeast

Asia that amounted to genocide. Since obedience to criminal law was no excuse at Nuremberg—and did not save Adolph Eichmann, a notorious Nazi official at his trial in Jerusalem—why, these resisters and evaders wished to know, should they be conscripted into an army bent upon a war its many opponents on the home front damned as literally atrocious, morally offensive, and legally indefensible? No one yet can answer this question. Yet human survival may well depend upon the answer to it and related questions of international law. For, as one expert, Edward J. Barrett, recently remarked:

> Progress in creating legal controls has only begun in the international field, but there is a widespread feeling that the science of destruction has so far preceded the science of international law that the nations of the world now must choose between mutual annihilation and law. Current headlines indicate both that the time for choice may be short and that the process of creating a viable international legal order will be incredibly complex and difficult—perhaps calling for a revolution in international political technology even greater and more complex than the revolution in scientific technology that brought us from gunpowder to hydrogen bombs.[5]

Meanwhile, the idea slowly advances that international law is "higher" than national law. By late 1970, our chief counsel at Nuremberg, General Telford Taylor, had written a book entitled *Nuremberg and Vietnam: An American Tragedy* in which he likened the massacre at My Lai to Nazi crimes against humanity. At the same time, political polarization continues. Activists of the extreme left and the extreme right feel that all law is subordinate to their lofty revolutionary or counter-revolutionary aims. And the old notion that God's law eclipses man's (although God's can be interpreted not only in divergent but in antipathetic terms) still holds sway over multitudes of people. The politics of assassination, usually tyrannicide, is as old as politics, hence as old as the state itself. From the assassin's point of view, his victim is the real criminal, who may or may not be so adjudged by his fellow citizens. Did criminal culpability lie with Brutus or with Caesar? With both? With neither? What shall

---

[5] "Police Practices and the Law—From Arrest to Release or Charge," in *The Sociology of Law*, ed. Rita James (San Francisco: Chandler, 1968), p. 438.

we say of the "good German" who obeyed Nazi laws that were personally abhorrent to him? Was he or his nonconformist comrade or Hitler with his thugs, his fiats, and his decrees, the most, the least, or not at all criminalistic? At any given time during Stalin's worst purges as many as fifteen million people, after having been summarily tried and convicted of mostly imaginary offenses, were deported to do slave labor in subhuman concentration camps where untold numbers of them perished. Were they or their judges the "true criminals"? As well ask whether the witches of Salem or the New England theocrats were more at fault, or which of them was more possessed, and by what, in colonial America.

Selective Access to Legal Rights

Jamestown, Cape Cod, and Roanoke Island are sufficiently perplexing to the social historian. What then can one make of Virginia and the Carolinas or the West Indies—all settled by freedom-loving Englishmen who as heirs of the Magna Carta and cocreators of the Enlightenment developed a system of chattel slavery as severe and cruel as any mankind has ever known? The Virginia gentlemen whose most eloquent spokesmen drew up the Declaration of Independence, chafing against the British crown, finally and illegally refused to pay taxes without parliamentary representation. Like the rum merchants, factors, and whalers to their north, southern planters were outraged at "unjust" restrictions imposed upon them by a distant royal personage who no longer commanded their allegiance. High treason was their crime, a capital offense that is graver than any other, and we honor them for it. They were republicans who sanctified the principle that all men are created equal. George Washington fully embodied, as Thomas Jefferson beautifully expressed, that principle. They were both slaveholders, perhaps reluctant, perhaps benevolent, but slaveholders all the same. Each was a party to the loathsome system by which human cargo was assembled in Africa, chained within the holds of ships, and brought to auction blocks for sale in a country that already prided itself on being the "land of the free and the home of the brave." The republicans, their blood lust whetted by violent revolution against other white men and decimation of the red men around them, proceeded to import black and brown men who were to be treated either as beasts of burden or as inanimate objects.

Given a libertarian and equalitarian ideology, adult human beings can be manacled, whipped, bludgeoned, debauched, patronized, mercilessly exploited, or simply slaughtered only if, upon stamping them as racially inferior, they are also adjudged to be less than human beings. Where did little England, still completely overshadowed by the Iberian colossus, get such an idea of exotic peoples; and how did their masters come to think of them as not much different from wildlife in general, as a conglomeration of nonpersons?

Throughout the mercantilist age, Western Europeans panted after bullion, seeking silver and gold as if in quest of the Holy Grail, ready to ransack the world for its possession. Five hundred years ago Spain and Portugal won that race, and to the victors went an empire. Modern imperialism came sooner even to Holland than to Britain, a small power turned in upon itself, engaged in internecine warfare, unready for aggrandizement and expansion. It would seem that contempt for the people about to be subdued is an essential component of the imperialist attitude. We cannot say how Britain acquired the necessary amount of contempt, but a neglected reason discussed by the American historian, Howard Mumford Jones, deserves our attention. Jones emphasized the example of Ireland, especially the struggles of sixteenth-century Englishmen to tame "the wild Irish." He writes:

> Though the English monopoly of gunpowder gave an overwhelming superiority to the royal forces, it became evident that mere military forays could not hold that country. If Ireland had never existed, the English in America would probably have refused to sell firearms to Indians who were "naked and unarmed, destitute of edged tools and weapons," but the immediacy with which British colonists were instructed to keep the natives unarmed suggests the pertinence of Irish experience.[6]

[6] *O Strange New World* (New York: Viking, 1967), p. 167.

The Glorification of Violence

Empire builders need to be historically conditioned for their mission. If they are to subdue, extirpate, enslave, or merely humiliate and hold another people, the proper frame of mind must be instilled in them. Britain was amply prepared, not only by its experience with the recalcitrant Irish, but in faraway places throughout the age of exploration. With other advantages, such as gun powder and the horse, to help induce a sense of superiority, new worlds could be conquered.

Presently, the American, that new breed of man, emerged; he was still rather isolated and parochial but basically no different from his predecessors. Spreading westward from the Atlantic Coast lay an apparently endless frontier. Covetous eyes were cast on its richness. Not until 1890 could that frontier be said to have achieved its uttermost extremes. Between the closing of the continental frontier and the First World War America embarked upon its only explicitly jingoistic and classically imperialistic adventure, one that resulted in the acquisition of overseas territories forcibly wrenched from a debilitated Spanish domain.

Many democratic institutions are partly traceable to the hardships of frontier life. They have been duly celebrated in a big corpus of romantic literature and nearly as big a corpus of scholarly history. Enforced egalitarianism unquestionably prevailed for an extended period under difficult circumstances in which a man's ability to track and hunt meant more than any amount of citified book learning. Guns truly were the "equalizers" that an underworld argot later labeled them. Mention of the frontier conjures up a great many disparate facets of our past. A gun mystique, beginning with the matchlock imported by Columbus, is common to many of them. Others are buried in hemispheric folklore. From the gauchos of Argentina to the cowpunchers of Texas, restless, fully armed, easily angered individualists are an irresistible staple of twentieth-century hero worship. Bat Masterson, Wild Bill Hickok, Wyatt Earp, Jesse James: those who ruthlessly broke the law and those who valiantly defended it are, in today's afterglow, equally estimable figures. That the outlaw and the sheriff should be equated is not just something seen darkly through a television glass, or brightly on the Vista Vision screen. The mass media reflect, even as they distort, a persistent social reality, namely that there is a certain kinship between good guys and bad guys, even between cops and robbers. It is not a kinship wholly peculiar to the United States.

More peculiar is our response to frontier conditions which, while comparable to those of say Australia or Canada, were so different in the milieux they produced. To those who have made guns a cult, most of them now organized in one of Washington's most powerful lobbies, the National Rifle Association, guns signify manhood. Not phallic potency and idealized masculinity with an overt sexual significance—which is the essence of Latin-American *machismo*— but their symbolic representation in side arms matter most in this strange tradition. Hence the apparent schizophrenia of citizens who today oppose gun-control legislation, which they damn as un-American, while vociferously condemning those who use guns to generate "crime on the streets." The era of gun-happy explorers, gamblers, Indian fighters, duelers, adventurers, rustlers, and train robbers as noble or ignoble frontiersmen is over, but in a way, it goes marching—and shooting—on. Pistols change: Bat Masterson's "peacemaker," a Colt .45, lovingly enshrined as "the gun that killed twenty-six badmen," was obviously more cumbersome than the Cloverleaf Colt and six shooter of a later day. They were all lethal enough, but their steady improvement and continued availability should guarantee that death by gunshot, underscored in high homicide and suicide rates, will not soon decline.

In a worshipful biography, circa 1931, of the legendary frontier marshal, Wyatt Earp, Stuart N. Lake writes:

> The frontier breeds men. Good or evil, law-abiding or lawless, the pick of the strain are fighting men. . . .
> For two sanguinary centuries in which North American civilization battled westward, Earps were in the vanguard of those hardy, self-reliant pioneers who led the course of empire across the wilderness. . . .
> Wyatt Earp, of the sixth American-born generation of his family,

was destined to a time and territory of which it was written that there was no law west of Kansas City and, west of Fort Scott, no God. . . .[7]

Can we doubt the accuracy of David Brion Davis, an American cultural historian, when he observed: "In general, Americans of the mid-twentieth century seem to think of themselves as a highly aggressive people who never commit acts of aggression, in spite of their imaginative interest in bloodshed"?[8] Davis continues:

> On the other hand, if we could formulate a generalized image of America in the eyes of foreign peoples from the eighteenth century to the present, it would surely include, among other things, a phantasmagoria of violence, from the original Revolution and Indian wars to the sordid history of lynching; from the casual killings of the cowboy and bandit to the machine-gun murders of racketeers. If America has often been considered a country of innocence and promise in contrast to a corrupt and immoral Europe, this sparkling, smiling, domestic land of easygoing friendliness, where it is estimated that a new murder occurs every forty-five minutes, has also glorified personal whim and impulse and has ranked hardened killers with the greatest of folk heroes. Founded and preserved by acts of aggression, characterized by a continuing tradition of self-righteous violence against suspected subversion and by a vigorous sense of personal freedom, usually involving the widespread possession of firearms, the United States has evidenced a unique tolerance of homicide.[9]

Davis is worth following a bit. He believes (and so does this writer) that certain literary conventions like the superman, the renegade, and the monomaniac have a psychological meaning that reflects fundamental social values. Whereas homicide in the abstract was always forbidden, those convicted of committing it were thought to have been diabolically possessed. Even in the nineteenth century, indictments for murder in the United States included this phrase: "Not having the fear of God before his eyes, but being moved and seduced by the instigations of the devil. . . ." Supernatural forces that presumably wove their aura of evil around a culprit, depriving

[7] *Wyatt Earp: Frontier Marshall* (Boston: Houghton Mifflin, 1931), p. 103.
[8] *Homicide in American Fiction, 1798–1860* (Ithaca, N.Y.: Cornell University Press, 1968), p. vii.
[9] Ibid., pp. vii–viii.

him of his will, were understood to be at fault. Nevertheless, a convicted murderer was, and still is, most often subject to the death penalty, which is to say, another act of murder. Not that the United States in matters pertaining to capital punishment has been especially savage. Under the aspect of eternity, its record is one of restraint. As Leonard Savitz recently remarked, "Criminals have been executed for at least 3,500 years by being stoned, decapitated, hanged, beaten, shot, electrocuted and gassed." [10] For what? "Death has been inflicted for such offenses as consorting with gypsies, singing scurrilous songs, and disobeying one's parents, as well as for the major felonies that have always been capital crimes." [11]

The picture is not a pretty one no matter when or where we look. Cruelty to real and alleged malefactors has never been in short supply. Few, if any, of the more advanced techniques originated in the United States, but sometimes they were refined into a distinctive American pattern. Davis's study concentrates on forms of revenge condoned in large parts of the United States from 1798 to 1860, specifically dueling and lynching. Each was justified as an expression of vengeance made necessary by righteous passion. Noting among Americans, particularly those in the South and West, "a violent sensitivity to insult," coupled with peculiar standards of gentlemanly honor—such that a prominent federalist lawyer, Thomas O. Selfridge, could describe that quality in 1807 to be "as sacred as a woman's virtue"—and a code that stemmed from it, extralegal violence became more or less mandatory. Smoothbore pistols, shotguns, bowie knives, and rope were socially sanctioned means by which certain disputes were customarily resolved. Davis hardly overstates the case when he reminds us that:

> From the end of the Revolution through most of the nineteenth century, Americans of the South and West accepted two outlets for aggression which differed significantly from even the more violent and brutal customs of Europe. Dueling which originated in the medieval Appeal and Wager of Battle to settle private wrongs, and which flourished in Europe in the form of secret and illegal combat, became, in America,

[10] *Dilemmas in Criminology* (New York: McGraw-Hill, 1967), p. 7.
[11] Loc. cit.

unrestrained and unregulated warfare. Unlike his European counterpart, the American duelist's principal objective was often to kill an enemy by any means whatsoever. Whereas dueling in Europe was confined to the upper classes who were more concerned with procedures and formalities than with actual killing, dueling in America was not limited by class distinctions. In the South and West the duelist impatiently tolerated and frequently dispensed with formal rules, since his purpose was mainly to annihilate or disable an enemy with as little ceremony as possible. Although lynching has been traced back to the feudal *Vehmgerichte*, there was nothing in eighteenth and nineteenth century Europe comparable to American lynch "law," which spread from colonial Virginia and Carolina to the South and West. Both of these aggressive practices were justified by an assumption that the people had only conditionally and temporarily surrendered their primitive right of retribution to legal representatives.[12]

Any list of circumstances conducive to the Americanization and brutalization of dueling, the vigilant spirit that fostered private but organized settlement of public grievances—from revolutionary Minutemen to reactionary Minutemen—and to the perpetuation of lynching preceded by torture, would be a long one. Davis mentions territorial and judicial power in frontier communities, increasing sectional conflicts, the presence of differing racial, religious, and ethnic groups, the rapid growth of cities, and the diffusion of industrialism. One could go on. Some of these circumstances have all but disappeared; others have been attenuated and transformed; yet others have been exacerbated. Whether in the background or in the foreground, all of them have a strong bearing on the crime question in America.[13]

[12] Davis, *Homicide in American Fiction*, p. 268.

[13] On August 16, 1968, Ramsey Clark, the attorney general of the United States, was reported in the *New York Times* to have deplored "loose talk of shooting looters" as likely to cause guerilla warfare between blacks and whites in American cities. He contended that, "No civilized nation in history has sanctioned summarily shooting thieves caught in the commission of their crime." He asked, "Will America be the first?" Addressing himself to a group of state trial judges, his text includes this striking passage (which takes us beyond the period surveyed by Davis): "A nation which permitted the lynching of more than 4,500 people, nearly all Negroes, between 1882 and 1930 can ill afford to engage in summary capital punishment without trial in our turbulent times."

Crime and Violence as Social Values

Davis points out that lynching, as an institutionalized, if localized, American rite (which could not be formally abolished by a southern-dominated United States Congress until the middle of this century) bore a close resemblance to the punishment of a renegade or an enemy spy. "The victim was an alienated man, often the representative of a scapegoat group, whose very existence infuriated a mob of righteous men." [14] He adds an insight that, despite its use of the past tense, has all kinds of contemporary relevance: "When Americans endeavored to establish law and order in new regions beset by racial conflict or by social and economic uncertainty, there often was a tendency for citizens to rise in mass violence in an attempt to achieve a clear and positive expression of group cohesion, authority and justice." [15]

In this period of extraordinary social and economic uncertainty, with its widespread moral anarchy, the tendency for citizens to rise in mass violence has assumed global proportions. A portentously growing stockpile of thermonuclear weapons is on hand in more than one world capital. Violence begets violence, direct action leads to massive repression in a deadly spiral that threatens the species with extinction. Both new and old regions are more beset by racial conflict than ever. Frontier lawlessness, with additional complications, has come to be the norm in many parts of the world. Our part is no longer separable from the rest. Black nationalism, for instance, has arisen in the United States not only as a separatist movement. It simultaneously seeks self-determination in an independent state or as a state within a state, and identification with blacks in Africa and elsewhere. The United States riot report of 1968 starkly specifies, "This is our basic conclusion: Our nation is moving toward two societies, one black, one white—separate and unequal." [16] That finding, as

[14] Ibid., pp. 272–73.
[15] Ibid., p. 273.
[16] *Report of the National Advisory Commission on Civil Disorders* (New York: Bantam Books, 1968), p. 1.

Tom Wicker says in his introduction to the report, comes from the considered judgment of moderate and "responsible" Establishmentarians. It is not wish-fulfillment voiced by "black radicals, militant youth or even academic leftists." [17] Indeed, the Commission, when appointed by President Johnson, was severely criticized for its conservative character. This nation is moving toward two societies, black and white superimposed upon the two separate but unequal societies it already contains, those of the rich and the poor. The entire human population is increasingly polarized into these divisions. Black, yellow, and white peoples, rich and poor nations, most of them ridden with internal discord that is a miniature of the larger reality: this is the broad context, these are the key variables from which we must try to apprehend crime in America. The full measure of ambiguity, fog, paradox, and dilemma, if not the nature and causes of a phenomenon no one has satisfactorily defined, can be specified and clarified. To the broad context and the key variables, an historical dimension must be added, and it must be kept constantly in mind.

Our own enigmatic, possibly post-Modern but as yet unnamed era has frequently been likened to that of Elizabethan England. It too was transitional and bewildering. Hiram Haydn finds Renaissance man, and not only in England, as ambivalent or as multivalent as twentieth-century man, and for much the same reason. Each was caught in a violent transition requiring sudden movement from an antecedent, rather stable but senile world view, to a still incohate post-Renaissance or post-Modern world view.[18] Such a transition can only be convulsive. It is much more dangerous this time, with race suicide and not merely the fall of civilization in prospect.

The Selective Application of Criminal Law

American law, criminal and civil, common and statutory, has always drawn heavily upon Anglo-Saxon precedent. Legal history shows

[17] Ibid., p. v.
[18] Hiram Haydn, *The Counter-Renaissance* (New York: Charles Scribner's Sons, 1958), passim.

continuity with, as well as affinity between, the British and American systems. Revolution, which establishes a new body of law, never means the total rupture that on-the-scene myopia makes it out to be. The Federal Constitution and the Bill of Rights are eighteenth-century documents drawn largely from British and continental jurisprudence. Direct legal links between Britain's time of troubles and our own can be demonstrated. Of these, none is more obvious than present-day welfare legislation in the American states and its origin in Elizabethan poor laws.

Loren Miller, a municipal judge in the city of Los Angeles, pinpointing this connection, concedes that welfare in the United States also has an indigenous overlay of humanitarianism, that it is brightened by occasional flashes of conscience, a weak and wavering sense that the richest nation on earth need not keep millions of its disadvantaged citizens below subsistence, and that chronic failure to nurture a meaningful proportion of the young or care for the ill and aged can be a costly public policy, intensifying the current strife and leading to more serious class confrontation. "Nevertheless," writes Judge Miller, "the ill, the handicapped, the aged, the jobless (after unemployment benefits are exhausted), the deserted mother, the fatherless child are often treated as beggars and mendicants at best or as rogues, vagabonds and vagrants, at worst. The welfare administrator who keeps as many applicants as possible out of benefits is in a fair way to win the approbation of his community and of its establishment." [19] Moreover:

> All too often rules are administered to exclude apparently qualified applicants, and every effort to utilize existing regulations in such a manner as to obtain benefits is branded as "fraud. . . ." Current mores condone, even honor, the rich taxpayer whose lawyers and accountants find loopholes in the law that enable him to avoid income tax payments, but the welfare recipient who finds a loophole that enables her to increase aid to her children is an object of public wrath. The taxpayer is entitled to whatever savings he can effect; the welfare recipient is not "entitled" to aid provided for him. [20]

[19] Loren Miller, "Race, Poverty and the Law," in *The Law of the Poor,* ed. Jacobus Ten Broek (San Francisco: Chandler, 1966), p. 73.
[20] Ibid., p. 65.

A conservative estimate of Americans below the poverty line, including more than ten million souls below the *subsistence* line—as this is written—would be about twenty-nine million. Mexican-Americans, Puerto Ricans, and other Latinos; North American Indians; Applachian whites; and the descendants of African tribesmen brought here as slaves constitute a disproportionately large part of the poor. In the majority of cases, race prejudice is a conspicuous element in the maladministration of criminal justice that impinges most heavily on our largest minority, the more than twelve million people who derive from the southern slavocracy formally dissolved more than a hundred years ago. Invidious racial distinctions, tolerated in the Constitution as originally interpreted by the Supreme Court, were forbidden by Civil War amendments. They were reinterpreted and reestablished thereafter, and most recently disestablished once again. The dignity of the individual and the inviolability of his rights apply, in constitutional language, to every individual as a *person*.

> The Constitution vindicated those principles for white Americans, but recognition and protection of slavery inflicted a mortal wound as far as the Negro was concerned. . . . The Constitution as construed and as applied imposed legal disabilities on the slave; he was stripped of his individual dignity simply because of his race and stood not as a *person* but as a slave before the law of the land.[21]

Even freedmen were not yet free men. So long as slavery lasted, neither the freeborn nor the emancipated Negro completely escaped the legal disabilities imposed on his slave kinsmen. Privileges graciously extended could and were arbitrarily withdrawn even after abolition. Reconstruction briefly provided such sweeping improvement that with the passage of a civil rights act in 1875, which sought to eradicate all legal inequities based on race and past conditions of servitude, Charles Sumner could proclaim: "Hereafter there shall be no such word as 'black' or 'white.' . . . We shall speak only of citizens and men." Today, with interracial tension greater than ever before, such a pronouncement would most likely elicit bitter and derisive laughter. What has been called the strange history of Jim

[21] Ibid., p. 75.

Crow followed Reconstructionist enlightenment. White America, north and south, healed its wounds, in part, by inflicting them on black America.

This crisis, from the first a disruptive and eruptive force in United States society, threatens to reach a new high in the near future. At times more or less quiescent, it has seldom been less than acute. Nor is any quick resolution of the American dilemma, with its irreconcilable differences between patriotic lore and actual practice, yet in sight. Juridical symptoms of the dilemma abound in every section of the land. They are most virulent in those states that composed the old Confederacy, but near at hand everywhere else in each stage of the system by which Americans criminalize certain of their compatriots. In the Deep South it has been customary to take four types of criminal justice for granted. Punishment tends to be meted out with excessive leniency if both the attacker and the victim are blacks, likewise if the attacker is white and the victim is black. Excessive harshness occurs if the attacker is black and the victim white. Barring other inequities (of which there are many), only when both attacker and victim are white can the rules of evidence and a closer approximation of due process come into play. Color blindness before the law is a majestic ideal whose violation by public officials is still the rule.

Judge Miller points to the manner in which *"Negro* illegitimacy" is made public by social workers who administer AFDC (Aid to Families with Dependent Children). In his opinion, dissemination of carefully kept statistics is used to reinforce racial stereotypes. He expresses his view that, "The Constitution is color blind when discrimination is practised against persons because of their race, but color-conscious when persons have special needs as a result of prior discrimination." Prior racial discrimination refers to a condition that obtained during the slavocracy. Black women were frequently reduced to the status of breeding mares, sexually available to spawn more slaves. Unlike the West Indian or South American slave family, which was generally preserved, the North American slave family was deliberately pulverized. That past condition has only been partially rectified. Public clamor against unwed mothers is directed largely at the progeny of generations of defenseless black women who were impregnated by their white masters. No legal responsibility for racially mixed offspring devolved upon the fathers.

What we have to do with, in one word, is a discriminatory racial classification within a discriminatory economic classification. This classification makes for discriminatory application, administration, and implementation of the criminal law. The poor are in a bind, the black poor doubly and trebly so. Policemen, bondsmen, prosecutors, judges, parole boards, probation officers, guards, wardens, and commissioners—not to exhaust the relevant cast of characters—all make it apparent that this nation, far from being one and indivisible, is at the very least divided into rich and poor, white and black. Many more fissures crack the myth of indivisibility, viz., those suggested by male-female, old-young, and urban-suburban differentiation. For the moment we can limit ourselves to saying that ethnically, economically, and in a host of other ways, this country is split into "The Two Nations" Benjamin Disraeli designated when he used that term as an alternative title for his novel *Sybil*, which depicts nineteenth-century English social life.

Michael Harrington did much in *The Other America*[22] to dispel the illusion of universal affluence. While informing his countrymen about poverty in America, Harrington himself was amazed at its magnitude. At a minimum, tens of millions of men, women, and children were involved. The poor "who are always with us" were no longer with us, for they had been banished in the 1950s from our predominantly middle-class consciousness. Instead of traditional degradation accompanied by stoical resignation, *invisibility* had been achieved. The poor, when no longer treated like things—as if they were an odd subhuman extrusion—simply disappeared. In census after census several million of them went uncounted, as an unknown number of their corpses went uncounted in foreign wars and urban riots. Lately they have made their presence felt. It is not now possible to ignore the cry whose message says in effect: "We're for real. You'd better believe it."

So many in the well-to-do middle class and the well-paid working

---

[22] Michael Harrington, *The Other America* (Baltimore: Penguin Books, 1968).

class do believe that panic and fear have overcome politically significant numbers of them. They are shaken by and frightened of a frustrated underclass occupying "pockets" of poverty that turn out to be larger than anyone imagined until activists like Harrington told them about it. Consequently, for more than a decade an overriding American domestic issue has been crime and its ostensible increase. The political catch phrases that make this matter a "gut issue" are "crime on the streets" and the "preservation of law and order." Often these phrases echo, while they mask and mute, the racists' impulse to destroy "them Niggers." And the words are so understood by a far-out right wing constituency of cryptographers who decode them in their own way. A certain portion of the more privileged, educated, and liberal public, without much or any racist taint, is simply scared—and conveys that feeling to leaders who are asked to provide better protection for them, for their families, and for their property. The other America, exuding that foreign matter that makes solid citizens so apprehensive of their personal safety and security, would somehow have to be contained. Accordingly, "conservatives" advocate repression, which when it does not work, prompts them to ask for more repression. "Liberals" favor elimination of the causes, but nobody really knows the causes; thus, when meliorative measures fail, they call first for further inquiry, and then for more meliorative measures. Such is the pass, or the impasse, in which this country finds itself as mankind approaches the last quarter of a turbulent century. Crime, whatever it is, has all of a sudden been defined in many quarters as our number one social problem. The full exploration of that astonishing fact would take us very far afield. A few sociological and metasociological reflections are, however, most apropos.

The Liberal Doctrine of Criminal Justice

Winston Churchill once said that the public attitude toward criminals constitutes "a sure test of the level of civilization." [23] If so, then these

[23] The reference is a famous one and appears in, among many other sources, the concluding chapter of a book by John B. Mays, *Crime and the Social Structure* (London: Faber and Faber, 1967), p. 228.

essentials of the liberal doctrine as set forth by criminologist Leon Radzinowicz should not be forgotten:

> Since law, and especially criminal law, placed restrictions upon individual freedom, there should be as little of it as possible. To prohibit an action unnecessarily increases rather than decreases crime. Moreover, it was not the function of the law to enforce moral virtue as such, but simply to serve the needs of a particular society. . . .
>
> As to the administration of justice: it was here above all that the individual had suffered most in the past and here that it was most necessary to build secure lines of defense against the encroachments of the state. . . . Presumption of innocence should be the guiding principle: the maxim, so fashionable at the beginning of the nineteenth century, that it is better that ten guilty persons escape than that one innocent man should suffer, tersely expressed this deeply felt concern.[24]

Men like Cesare Beccaria and Wilhelm von Humboldt (who believed that the evils occasioned by police regulations outweighed those they prevented) set forth a general position that not even its Western heirs can take for granted. Those who hold this position declare that insofar as a society attempts to legislate sin out of existence, seeking thereby to govern private morals by criminal law, it reverses the historic trend away from tyranny. If this assertion is construed as a pure value judgment, which some of us view also as a demonstrable fact, no one need feel constrained to accept it. That the criminalization of many common acts helps to account for our crime problem is another matter.

The Totalitarian Potential

This argument has taken two contemporary American criminologists to a point where they see current police practice as the bearer of a serious totalitarian potential. Jerome H. Skolnick and J. Richard Woodward offer their empirical findings to underscore a real and present danger.[25] They realize how easily the delicate legal fabric can be torn apart when law becomes the major device for impos-

[24] *Ideology and Crime* (London: Heinemann, 1966), p. 2.
[25] "Bureaucracy, Information and Social Control," in *The Police*, ed. David J. Bordua (New York: John Wiley and Sons, 1967), pp. 99–136.

ing conventional morality. To a large extent the police, who are our official guardians of that morality, have been prevented from achieving full success, or total competence, by their very human limitations. Even now, it is impossible for them to be everywhere; nor are they Argus-eyed agents of the conformist behavior that society theoretically demands.

The police have always needed to persuade, pay, threaten, or coerce informants to help them gather intelligence. Perfected or not, any system of surveillance and enforcement consisting solely of human contacts, is necessarily fallible. So long as we rely only on people for the production of incriminating evidence, most so-called immorality goes undetected, unprosecuted, and consequently, unpunished. But as police efficiency increases, the crime rate looks more alarming, and totalitarian control draws closer. The puny human factor diminishes before an awesome technology.

Skolnick and Woodward draw our attention not only to new means for observing and recording transgressions—hidden binoculars, wiretaps, high-power binoculars—but also to the computerized and centralized information they supply. Data banks with instant retrieval that may include police, court, probation, school, welfare, and health records are already underway.

Skolnick and Woodward address themselves to one small but paradigmatic situation in the state of California. There, statutory rape is an offense that occurs when a man has sexual intercourse with a willing girl under the age of eighteen, who is not his wife. At the time of this study, no allowance was made if the male honestly and with reason believed the girl to be over the age of consent. Since a 1964 California Supreme Court decision, People *vs.* Hernandez, the defendant may plead that he mistakenly but in good faith took the girl to be eighteen years of age or older. The research is concerned with all statutory rapes reported in two jurisdictions: that of the Westville Police Department between January 1962, and October 1963 (a total of 235 cases), and for comparative purposes, that of a nearby community, Mountain City, where 87 cases were reported for the year 1961. The population of Mountain City is larger than that of Westville. Nevertheless, for the period studied, more cases of statutory rape were reported in Westville than in Mountain City where, for instance, 40 cases came to the attention of the police in 1961. Skolnick and Woodward explain this difference as the statistical artifact that it is. Available figures grossly distort both the incidence and the distribution of an offense whose actual magnitude we cannot know. Those in the upper and middle reaches of American society are not given to lodging complaints that would reveal the sexual indiscretions of their offspring. Parents from the lowest stratum of that society, though they may appear somewhat less reluctant, are also not overeager to act as complainants. Yet it is this stratum, and not only in a corner of California, that supplies most of the known-because-reported cases. Then, why the difference between Westville and Mountain City in numbers and in racial composition (67 percent Negroes compared to 22 percent white)? More Negroes live in Westville, but not enough to account for the disproportionate ratios. In a meticulous examination of the police process, Skolnick and Woodward reveal many pertinent details, and of these one emerges as decisive:

> The Mountain City family support division does not systematically report violations it discovers while taking welfare applications, and it is largely to this difference that the different outcome is attributable. . . . As a result, many of the features of the Westville cases are lacking in Mountain City: fewer reporting persons wait until they are certain the girl is pregnant before reporting the offense . . . ; offenses are reported more quickly . . . ; and Negroes are involved in far fewer of the cases. . . .[26]

One agency in possession of facts otherwise unavailable to the public passes them on to another agency. If A tells B, and B—using its broadly discretionary powers of enforcement—decides to prosecute, nonvoluntary complainants are found, and statutory rape looks like a serious matter. Actual fluctuation in rates remain unknown and unknowable, but when information about welfare recipients is exchanged with police officials, a larger than ordinary number of these people will be included as offenders. Hence for the record, poor men have a far greater propensity to commit acts of statutory rape than rich men. Where this reporting system has yet to be adopted,

[26] Ibid., p. 111.

the propensity is officially less pronounced. The system implies an increase in police efficiency that will be further facilitated by improved technology. It exposes much that would remain unexposed about the "wicked ways" of those in an affluent society who receive public assistance. Skolnick and Woodward concluded that the Westville policeman is significantly more successful than his Mountain City counterpart in locating "crime," not because of his superior skill nor his more rational administration, but because he taps welfare records.

These criminologists believe that for their kind of data, Philip Selznick has posed the most appropriate question, namely: "Do we need or want agencies of control so efficient and so impartial that every actual offender has an equal chance of being known and processed?" [27] Selznick's question answers itself in the negative. For a condition where every offender has an equal chance of being known and "processed" presupposes the politicization, criminalization, and totalitarianization of everything. We are some distance from that extremity. So far it is only a criminological nightmare that threatens to materialize as mechanical detection replaces merely human effort in order to maintain "law and order." If instant exposure and swift punishment followed the commission of all acts defined at this moment as violations of existing statutes, then our society would be nothing but an enormous prison. One cannot dismiss either Selznick's disturbing question or his implicit answer. Yet I greatly doubt whether that question is the right one. Skolnick and Woodward have shown that consequential public policy can be set when welfare department records are transmitted by a family support division to police officials. Specially created to uncover fraud and nonsupport, the family division may be instrumental in reporting crimes outside its sphere.

The authors ask us to consider what would happen if public policy of this sort extended into other institutional spheres. They offer public schools as an example: "Many acts routinely dealt with by school officials under the label of school discipline—petty theft, carrying of knives, assaults, sport 'pools'—could conceivably be re-

[27] "Foundations of the Theory of Organization," *American Sociological Review* (February 1948), p. 84.

ported to the police for criminal processing." [28] And so they are—
not always, or the public schools would be depopulated, but often
enough to help overcrowd nearly every reformatory and training
school in the land. These offenses, petty theft and so forth, cover a
large part of juvenile delinquency.

The urban public school year by year comes closer to being synonymous with the slum school, in contrast to the private school, the
parochial school, and the suburban white school; it is filled with
children who learn soon enough that they belong to persecuted
minorities. Today's public school is one of many conduits through
which some of these children are remanded to punitive and "re-
habilitative" agencies where detention rather than education or
correction is the rule. Social critics like Paul Goodman regard the
average public schol as an institution very much like a penal colony.
If still more police discipline is substituted for the fairly rigid school
discipline that already prevails, then an even larger number of dark,
or not so dark, and impoverished youth will be caught directly in
the coils of the law. Far from attaining impartial justice such that
"each actual offender has an equal chance" of being apprehended
and punished, we would achieve a marked enlargement of the discriminatory treatment chronically accorded underdogs. That such
criminal justice shows no sign of abatement is a major component
in the strife besetting America.

The "Record" and Its Effect on Employability

We cannot overemphasize this point: discriminatory treatment before the law in a formal framework of equality weighs heavily, op-
pressively, and among both victims and offenders, more consciously
than ever, on the poor. The poor, moreover, are likely to discover
that unhappy truth early in life. Unlawful conduct, *which results in
arrests and adjudication,* is overwhelmingly found among the young.
Teen-agers and subteen-agers, not deemed to have reached the age
of reason, are technically irresponsible. Special courts exist to pro-

[28] Skolnick and Woodward, in Bordua, *The Police,* p. 112.

tect them from being branded as criminals. They and slightly older youths comprise the hard core of our highly publicized crime problem. Given a national population nearly half of which was born after 1945, those in the sixteen to twenty-one bracket are by far the largest criminal category. On this datum all authorities are agreed—as they are agreed on the low socioeconomic status of most youthful offenders. To be pigeonholed as offenders, they must first have been convicted. Mere arrest cannot be equated with guilt, especially when, "According to a recent estimate based on 1963 F.B.I. crime reports, approximately two and one-half million persons arrested annually for non-traffic offenses are *not* convicted," [29] Edward V. Sparer who cites this estimate, goes on to say, "Despite the court's finding that such persons are not guilty, social punishment for the *fact of arrest* is often quick to follow." [30] He quotes from a New York City Advisory Council memorandum which in his opinion accurately describes one countrywide form of inequity:

> The major handicap from an arrest record appears to be in securing and retaining employment, membership in a labor organization, or apprenticeship training. Applications for both public and private employment sometimes ask whether an applicant has ever been convicted, but also whether he has ever been arrested or charged, and sometimes even whether he has ever received a summons. . . .
>
> The persons most affected by this practice are almost invariably those who reside in disadvantaged areas, of whom a high proportion are Negroes and Puerto Ricans. Wholesale arrests of "suspects" on vagrancy charges are often made when a crime or a "rumble" has occurred in a high delinquency area. Most of these "suspects" are released after questioning, but their job opportunities have been endangered without any proof of guilt. . . .[31]

The disadvantaged boy living in a so-called high-delinquency area may seem disrespectful, uppity, mischievous, or idle. The policeman, who enjoys a social status higher than that boy and his family, must decide whether or not to include him in a round-up of "sus-

---

[29] Edward V. Sparer, "Employability and the Juvenile 'Arrest' Record," in *Work, Youth, and Unemployment,* eds. Melvin Herman, Stanley Sadofsky, and Bernard Rosenberg (New York: Thomas Y. Crowell, 1968), p. 470.

[30] Loc. cit.

[31] Loc. cit.

pects." If he chooses to make the "pinch," it will be a first arrest in about one case out of four. Guarantees of confidentiality and anonymity notwithstanding, this experience can blight the rest of the boy's life. Arrested, booked, interrogated, and discharged as innocent, he now has a "record," ostensibly unavailable to others who represent a society that wishes to protect him even if his behavior *has* been judged wrongful or harmful. The statutory language in New York is similar to that of other jurisdictions: ". . . no person adjudicated a juvenile delinquent . . . shall be denominated a criminal by reason of such adjudication." Further: "All police records relating to the arrest and disposition of any person under this article . . . shall be withheld from public inspection." Loopholes are specified. "Such records shall be open to inspection upon good cause shown by the parent, guardian, next friend, or attorney of that person upon written order of a judge of the family court in the county in which the order was made or, if the person is subsequently convicted of a crime, of a judge of the court in which he was convicted." [32]

These exceptions do not include possibly prejudiced employers, union leaders jealously guarding the ethnic exclusivity of their membership, or personnel in nonjudicial branches of the federal government. All are barred, as are neighbors, pressmen, and laymen at large, from scrutiny of presumably private and confidential documents. And all have fairly free access to them. Job applicants, as well as would-be apprentices and soldiers with "records," can lie about their past, which is itself an actionable practice, or they can compromise themselves by admitting the truth. Alternatively, young people sign waivers to their legal right of confidentiality. Privileged information is released, legislative intent is contravened, and anyone who in his minority was justly or unjustly *charged* with an offense can be incriminated.

Sparer emphasizes the abuse, not to say the impropriety and near illegality that most heavily penalizes young people who, in any event, are three or four times less employable than their more advantaged peers. Years ago, Austin Porterfield, a distinguished criminologist,

[32] Ibid., p. 472.

found no statistically significant difference between the waywardness of court children and college or precollege students. He defined the official delinquent as a friendless youth, moving under maximum conditions of exposure to arrest, usually on the street because there was no other place for him to be.[33] Such youths are hauled into station houses where their names appear on police blotters. Later on, out of school and out of work, countless numbers of them are disqualified from employment, from job training, and from service in the Armed Forces because they are held to be "poor risks"—with "records" they cannot erase.

The difficulties of slum-bred youth are thus compounded. Private employers, craft unions, and sections of the government disqualify precisely those whose employability is in the first place most restricted. It is usually considered too risky to hire these "potentially dangerous" criminals. Sparer reports a study made by the New York Civil Liberties Union of employment agency practices, in which fully 75 percent of the agencies sampled ask job applicants about arrest records, and, as a matter of regular and automatic procedure, would not refer those with arrest records irrespective of any judicial determination that may have been made. Adjudication of "delinquency," "youthful offender," and "wayward youth" are supposed to be purely civil and never criminal proceedings. The perversion of this principle exercises thoughtful judges, legal philosophers, and criminologists.

Protection of the Individual

Every few months crime is reported to be on the upswing, but it is not accidental that the full force of penal and social sanctions falls only on some offenders. The regular upswing can be partially attributed to greater efficiency in detecting and recording crime committed not just by any citizen. When two humane criminologists, Richard R. Korn and Lloyd W. McCorkle, ask, "How far may the state go in enforcing social values?" they correctly perceive ethical

[33] Austin C. Porterfield, "Delinquency and Its Outcome in Court and College," *American Journal of Sociology* (November 1943), pp. 199–208.

issues that transcend crime and punishment. One can only agree with them that, "To press for unlimited enforcement efficiency is, in effect, to assert that the ends justify the means. To set limits on the reaches of the law is, in effect, to assert that the individual is himself a social end." [34] The inference is valid and humanistic; sociologists can only salute the praiseworthy sentiment that underlies it. But once again, as with Selznick, sight has been lost of a differential, selective, and invidious process. No one presses for unlimited enforcement efficiency. Those who press wish to achieve greater and greater efficiency in the same limited area of class and race that has never ceased to be their concern.

Korn and McCorkle, in passages immediately preceding their critical question, draw upon a prominent legal authority, William Seagle, who neatly circumscribes the area. Seagle finds most justices of the Supreme Court of the United States expounding the view that efficiency in criminal law enforcement is irreconcilable with decency and liberty—which, in the profoundest sense, renders it unconstitutional. He sees the open exposition of this philosophy in Justice Jackson's statement that, "The forefathers, after consulting the lessons of history, designed our Constitution to place obstacles in the way of a too permeating police surveillance, which they seemed to think a greater danger to a free people than the escape of some criminals from punishment." [35] Except for an additional appraisal, this could still relate to unlimited efficiency. The key paragraph follows:

> Power can be curbed only by making the law inefficient. Indeed, the establishment of every limitation upon political power has been a tacit recognition of the undesirability of legal efficiency. Humanity has constantly drawn back from legal efficiency as from the brink of an abyss. When threatened by efficient law enforcement, it has loudly demanded Twelve Tables, codes, bills of rights, declarations of the rights of man, and full-fledged constitutions—*all for the purpose of protecting the weak against the strong, and the individual against the state.* In short it has always demanded inefficiency as an inalienable right of man. Of course, no one literally demands "inefficiency," which

[34] Richard R. Korn and Lloyd W. McCorkle, *Criminology and Penology* (New York: Holt, Rinehart and Winston, 1959), p. 97.

[35] Ibid., p. 96.

as an ideal has always been in bad odor. Everyone actually demands "liberty." Liberty, however, is only inefficiency in false face. (My italics.)[36]

"Protecting the individual against the state" is without any possible respite a matter of the utmost urgency. Safeguards built into criminal law are a political shield against authoritarian and totalitarian rule. So long, however, as democratic forms persist and we continue to cherish them, protecting the weak against the strong must remain uppermost in our minds. In the first instance, every full-blown twentieth-century dictatorship, whether of the right or the left, has taught us anew how heavily civil liberty and the principle of legality depend upon criminal law. That much should have been learned by anyone who has lived through or reflected upon the past fifty years of world history. Once in power, the Bolsheviks, the Nazis, the Maoists, and the Fidelistas, having enjoyed such civil liberty as they found (sometimes a great deal, sometimes very little), destroyed every vestige of the rights on which they had capitalized.

Over two decades ago, Jerome Hall summed up several traits common to authoritarian movements:

> Special police are exempt from legal constraint: they arrest, try, execute and exile without legal restraint. Appeal is limited or non-existent. Special tribunals for the trial of political offenders may be depended upon to effectuate the will of the government. There is sweeping abrogation of constitutional guarantees. All of this is rationalized and sustained by controlled philosophical thought, as interpreted by the leaders to implement their political aims. . . . Thus, during revolution, law, especially criminal law, is used as a party weapon.[37]

And, we may say that this is still so long after the revolution has run its course.

Hall refers us to the Russian Penal Code of 1926 which stated that:

> A crime is any socially dangerous act or omission which threatens the foundations of the Soviet political structure and that system of law which has been established by the Workers' and Peasants' Government for the period of transition to a Communist structure.

[36] Ibid., pp. 96–97.
[37] *General Principles of Criminal Law* (Indianapolis: Bobbs-Merrill, 1947), p. 57.

In cases where the Criminal Code makes no direct reference to particular forms of crimes, punishments or other measures of social protection are applied in accordance with crimes most closely approximating, in gravity and in kind, to the crimes actually committed. . . .[38]

Similarly, in Nazi Germany, the Act of June 28, 1935, provided that:

Any person who commits an act which the Law declares to be punishable or which is deserving of penalty according to the fundamental conceptions of penal law and sound popular feeling, shall be punished. If there is no penal law directly covering an act, it shall be punished under the law of which the fundamental conception applies most nearly to the said act.[39]

The arbitrariness this act exudes lasted only as long as National Socialism. Its spirit, by which the rule of law was temporarily expunged for Germans, has proved to be more durable in Soviet Russia. Fifty-one years after the October Revolution, James Reston, writing from Russia for the *New York Times* on November 21, 1968, noted: "Moscow has its own 'law and order.' If justice is 'incidental' to order, as J. Edgar Hoover is reported to have said the other day, he would be happy in Moscow. This is a policeman's paradise, and 'crime in the streets' is manageable."

At this writing the United States has still declined to opt fully for such law and order as Moscow confers on a disenfranchised citizenry. No higher priority has yet totally eclipsed or absolutely subordinated that concept of justice which runs like a golden thread through British and American law. Those who have not collapsed into totalitarianism, like those who have wrenched themselves free from its confinement, are better protected in their struggle for "the individual against the state" than they are in their struggle for "the weak against the strong." Pending a politically calamitous resolution of our many social and economic crises, which would involve our suspending the Constitution and the Bill of Rights, we are markedly more vulnerable on the second score than on the first.

[38] Ibid., p. 42.
[39] Loc. cit.

The Historical and Prehistorical Background

Before suprafamilial control of centralized state authority came into being, when man's existence was still coterminous with the band, the clan, and the tribe, reparation and revenge were identical. Attacker and defender, criminal and victim, and their kindred, all governed by an unshakable belief in collective and consanguineous responsibility, implicated one another in endless acts of retaliation. Every grave offense directed at an individual was also aimed at his whole clan or tribe: extended families avenged themselves on extended families as retaliation followed upon retaliation. Most important in primitive or preliterate and early Western law was that, "Injury was scaled in accordance with the seriousness of the trespass and the social evaluation of the aggrieved party." [40] Whoever attacked also provoked defense and counterattack—setting two families in motion, touching off a vendetta or blood feud. (The term, blood feud suggests kinship, which always mattered most, rather than bloodshed, which was often present.) Punishment was carefully graded to the litigant's social position.

This theme is the subject matter of all sagas, of all epic literature whether that of nomadic tribesmen or more settled peoples like the ancient Greeks, Romans, Icelanders, Gauls, and Anglo-Saxons. Gradually the blood feud gave way to other forms of reparation, "composition," or compensation. Survivals of the very old tradition remain in virtually every society, including our own. How could it be otherwise when, "The blood feud in Anglo-Saxon society was as central to social life as employment and taxes are today." [41] By modern standards, the violence of medieval Europe was prodigious. In the end, it must have been too enervating and too dangerous to be borne. With plague and hunger never far behind, only so much manslaughter, murder, and robbery-by-stealth could remain unchecked. An alternative to the blood feud, a legal process, had to be worked

[40] Norman F. Cantor, *The English* (New York: Simon and Schuster, 1968), p. 33.

[41] Ibid., p. 16.

out. Christendom, of which Briton was a part after the seventh century, sorely needed an authority both broader and more powerful than that of angry kinsmen. It was on this social necessity that Anglo-Saxon society founded the folk or community court.

From the late sixth century onward, a folk court or moot operated, at least among the leading warrior class in the small kingdoms of Kent, Wessex, Northumbria, and Mercia. It endured until Anglo-Norman time and then, in uneven stages after 1066, spread to all the indigenous Anglo and Saxon nations. By the eighth century, moots were differentiated into local courts called hundreds, and others encompassing subkingdoms or whole kingdoms, which were designated as shires. Historian Norman F. Cantor graphically describes how they worked:

> Whether it was the hundred or the shire court, the leading men of the community presided and arrived at decisions by a kind of consensus of the meeting. These leaders of the court may be called doomsmen or elders or wisemen but in all cases they were inevitably the men of greater substance and influence whose task was to work out and perpetuate legal processes in accordance with customary law. In the case of the hundred court the elders of the court could be ordinary peasants; in the case of the shire court they would always be the great warlords in the community. The first task of the folk moot was to build upon the old Germanic tradition that the blood feud could be abrogated in return for monetary compensation, the *Wergeld* (literally, man-money), to the dead man's kin. The kin were not required to take the wergeld and waive the right of revenge; it was the first obligation of the court to urge them to accept it. It was their second task to prepare lists of wergelds for every possible kind of violence, from the loss of a toenail, to the killing of a slave, to the killing of a nobleman or a king (the king's wergeld was placed so high that no man, no matter how many cattle he owned, could afford to pay it).[42]

The folk moot was designed to inhibit and, if possible, to abolish the exercise of family vengeance. It sought, without the sophistication of Roman law—which left no perceptible mark on early Britain—to determine who committed murder and robbery by stealth. Neither the rules of evidence nor rational procedure for the interrogation of witnesses had come into being. Moots reached a verdict

[42] Ibid., p. 37.

by invoking divine guidance as it was made manifest in the ordeal and by compurgation. A defendant was unlikely to survive the ordeal of hot iron or the ordeal of cold water. In the former, he touched a piece of red-hot iron, and if after three days his hand showed signs of festering, he was promptly hanged. England, with its many lakes and streams, seems to have favored the ordeal of water, in which the defendant, bound hand and foot, was flung into a body of water. "If he sank he was innocent and if he floated he was guilty, on the premise that water, being a holy element, would not receive a guilty man. The defendant thus had a choice between probable death by drowning and certain death by hanging." [43]

The historical record shows refinements and variations (the use of boiling cauldrons from which stones had to be retrieved, or two- and threefold ordeals), but in essence this was the judicial process. Christian churchmen initially found it repugnant, but while they added oaths and efforts to extract confessions, the ordeal had become so essential a part of Anglo-Saxon life that it could not be extirpated. Cantor argues that the folk court provided an element of rationality: "Only those defendants were put to the ordeal who were either commonly suspected of guilt"—which is an element of rationality— "or were of the lower social strata"—which is something else. Cantor informs us that, "It was a process almost exclusively designed for those who were peasants or who were 'ill-famed,' which to the medieval mind with its strong class biases meant almost the same thing." Then the historian cannot refrain from ruminating upon what he has just written: "Those who are horrified by this deep social prejudice might reflect on the kinds of people who have suffered capital punishment in the United States, noting the overwhelming proportion of Negroes and poor people. In this respect we have remained faithful to the traditions of Anglo-Saxon law." [44]

As long as society is somehow divided into the noble and the ignoble (which is to say, always and everywhere, and with or without ideological support), special provision must also be made for those of wealth and eminence. In this too we have remained faithful to

[43] Loc. cit.
[44] Loc. cit.

the tradition of Anglo-Saxon law. Compurgation against indictments in the folk court were for noblemen what ordeals were for peasants. Again, divine intercession was called for but in a much less exacting and arduous manner than the harsh method reserved for the common populace. In compurgation, the defendant swore to his innocence, and oath-helpers, graded by their wergelds, swore that his oath could be taken as "clean," in other words, that he was a man of good repute.

The court could decide only who should have the privilege of compurgation and how weighty the oath-helpers needed to be. As Cantor writes:

> Beyond this, a rich man who was oblivious to the heavenly perils of perjury and who had powerful relatives and friends of like dispositions could commit murder and robbery with impunity. He might be dealt with by the kin of the victim, but the court could not convict him. Thus Anglo-Saxon process tended to provide one procedure for the rich and the powerful and another for the poor and the unknown.

It is an understatement to conclude, "This class bias in somewhat less flagrant forms was to have a long history in English law and has not entirely ended at the present time." [45] Class bias, complicated by race, never ceased to operate. More opaque, subdued, and genuinely humane in the modern era, its recrudescence is apparent as crime becomes a public obsession.

How It Changes and Yet Remains the Same

The idea of individual autonomy was alien to all feudal law. Subjects, not yet citizens, were theoretically divested of will: they could only obey. In a strict hierarchical order thought to be ordained by Almighty God, no inferior could legitimately bring any accusation against a superior. Subjects were not entitled to invoke the help of a law court except against those of equal or subordinate status. In the feudal theocracy, no layman could charge a cleric with any

---

[45] Loc. cit.

crime. Walter Ullman, the eminent medievalist, has shown that in terms of ecclesiastical and secular law *people* of any age were defined as minors, requiring the undisputed protection of their overall superiors who in turn had been deputized by God to act *in loco parentis*. And what of the folk court? Ullman's answer is, "One can best understand the *Munt* (moot) if one compares it to the guardianship of a child: it is the kind of protection which a father affords to a child, or a guardian to his ward, or in Anglo-Saxon and Anglo-Norman England, the husband to his wife." [46]

High treason could be committed only against the king, or rather against his "highness," his *majestas,* a term pointing to the sublime office and function of him who was major. No royal *persona* could, and where the monarchy survives none can today commit a crime. By the same token, no mere vassal, but only a subject could commit high treason. "Petty treason" was of a lower order: it consisted in murder of the master by his servant, murder of the bishop by a clerk or a layman of his diocese, and murder of the husband by the wife. A remnant of old Roman law, elaborated by medieval jurists, namely, "What pleases the prince has the force of law," is quoted in modern canon law to this day. In a unique blend of Hellenistic, Roman, and Christian elements, the High Middle Ages produced a high legal synthesis. By it, law, already apotheosized in the invisible ruler, was literally embodied in the visible ruler. An organic, functional, collectivist metaphor, precluding any such modern idea as individual citizenship, underlay the whole conception. "The body politic" and related imagery, as the political scientist Michael Walzer has pointed out, served to justify a theoretically rigid hierarchy of persons that gradually supplanted the chaos of feudal arrangements:

> . . . as the head rules the body, medieval writers argued, so God the world and the king the polity; as the angels stand below in nine ranks and orders, so the nobler parts of the body politic below the king and the priests of the body of Christ below the Pope.[47]

[46] *The Individual and Society in the Middle Ages* (London: Methuen, 1967), p. 21.

[47] Michael Walzer, *The Revolution of the Saints* (New York: Atheneum, 1968), p. 7.

Walzer maintains that the inequality thus defended also established persistent patterns of obedience and deference. His conclusion is unexceptionable. And yet the curious system that comprises so large a part of our cultural heritage carried with it in embryonic form what we today would call the rule of law. Once again we see the sociological dialectic turn and turn about. The premodern world (and a whole assortment of metaphysical underpinnings) had to decompose before the rule of law could become a widely held ideal. For awhile, with the spread of equalitarianism from Western Europe, the ideal seemed to have triumphed. Actually, in waxing and waning, its precarious nature is clearly exposed.

At best the rule of law never fully banished inequality before the law. A veteran English magistrate, John Watson, reflecting on his long career, finds it most appropriate in 1969 to use as the epigraph to a book of selected memoirs this passage from *King Lear*, act 4, sc. 6:

See how yon' justice rails upon yon' simple thief.
Hark, in thine ear: change places; and, handy-dandy,
which is the justice, which is the thief? [48]

By and large, and handy-dandy, Shakespeare's fool knew enough to ask the question without which no criminological answer is worth a moment's notice.

For Further Consideration

1. To what extent and in what ways is crime a result of the operation of society?
2. How is the notion of a higher law related to crime?
3. To what extent do governments foster crime and violence? Explain.
4. To what extent are crime and violence part of our culture and our social values?
5. How is crime related to political power?
6. What is the relationship between crime and morality?
7. Is police efficiency desirable? Discuss.
8. How is crime related to concepts of equality before the law?

[48] John Watson, *Which Is the Justice?* (London: George Allen and Unwin, 1969), epigraph.

I N WESTERN thought, the number three exercises a persistent fascination. Its roots are perhaps to be found in the Christian trinity; classical scholars can point to earlier adumbrations. We periodize our history into ancient, medieval, and modern. An ecumenical historian like Oswald Spengler or Arnold Toynbee who rejects these conventional categories, invents a triad of his own and projects it onto the whole world. The eschatological Hegelian dialectic is composed of a thesis countered by its antithesis, culminating in a synthesis that sets the cycle going again. Philosophers, theologians, historians, psychologists, and sociologists keep ringing their own variations on this theme. How many social classes are there? Why, three. Everyone knows there are upper, middle, and lower classes. When a social scientist like W. Lloyd Warner and his associates took exception to this common-sense division, they simply subdivided the accepted classes. Thus Warner discerned not just an upper class but an upper-upper and a lower-upper class, not just a middle but an upper-middle and lower-middle class, not just a lower but an upper-lower and lower-lower class. The result was a six-class system: not three but twice times

7

Stability and Change

three. The pristine number begat an identical number, and remained intact.[1]

Sociology was launched under the banner of Auguste Comte's powerful and memorable triad, according to which mankind passed from the religious stage, through the metaphysical stage to the positive or scientific stage. Most Social Darwinists of the same era proclaimed ex cathedra that mankind passed from savagery through barbarism to civilization. All of culture, reified and uncontaminated by people or the choices they might make, was assumed to undergo the same sequential evolution. Indeed the identical evolutionary principle was applied to every separate culture and to the structure of its language, its kinship system, its technological, magical, and religious makeup. Some Social Darwinists reconstructed savagery by painting it in horrid tints and hues; others viewed this and the subsequent stages they commonly postulated through rose-colored glasses. Few doubted the truth-value of their conventional wisdom.

We have touched on other triadic schemes such as Jean Piaget's, which carries the individual from theocracy through gerontocracy to democracy. David Riesman's three-fold saga depicts man as once tradition-directed, then inner-directed, and finally other-directed— with "autonomy" hovering somewhere in the wings, waiting to join with, or eclipse, each basic form. None of these schematic arrangements, taken literally, will sustain close textual analysis. Man is too refractory in all ages to be so neatly pigeonholed. I think nevertheless that this kind of conceptualization is worthwhile. It is especially instructive if we shift the emphasis from sequence to simultaneity.

Was man long ago, as Comte insisted, a religious creature and nothing else? Did he cease to be religious in the eighteenth century only to become a complete metaphysician? Has metaphysics disappeared as positivism totally usurped its position? Comte gives indications here and there that he knew better. All that Clio vouchsafes from the past, combined with what we can grasp about ourselves in the present, leaves us with a portrait of man as a being who through all his vicissitudes has been what he is: at one and the same time,

---

[1] Lloyd Warner and Paul S. Lunt, *The Social Life of a Modern Community* (New Haven, Conn.: Yale University Press, 1941). This is the first of many volumes written or inspired by Warner.

religious, metaphysical, and scientific. We could never have relied simply on spirits, ghosts, or gods. Believing in them, man also looked after himself. Did he all of a sudden develop metaphysical abstractions? Or is every noun in every language, as the linguists tell us, a metaphysical abstraction? Can any science except a deluded positivism do without its metaphysical foundations? Only on the day that Bishop Berkeley and David Hume are definitively refuted. On that day the existence of an external world and the reality of causation will be demonstrated. Until then science must continue to take for granted what it cannot and need not demonstrate. And we in our everyday lives, using the same pragmatic test, will do likewise. Some societies are more secular than others, some more sacred; some encourage metaphysics, others do not; some apply science more than others; and all tend to be peopled with human beings who are composites of Comte's three stages.

Is it basically any different with Piaget's three stages of development? Let us concede that the child is at first a true believer, a full-blown theocrat, that in time he becomes a gerontocrat passively submitting to the authority of his elders, and that somewhat later he emerges for good from his cocoon, an independent democrat, ready to join his peers in destabilizing and restabilizing the culture into which they are all inducted. What is the upshot? What, finally, is man if not an endlessly varied mixture of theocratic, gerontocratic, and democratic components? If we are never altogether free or autonomous, neither are we ever altogether unfree or heteronomous.

Try it once more, this time with David Riesman's three world-historical stages. No one can quarrel with the "ideal types," the constructs against which we seek to measure degrees of fit or congruence. On comparison, some societies and some individuals are more tradition-directed, more inner-directed, or more other-directed. But where is the individual or the society devoid of all three motivational forces? And even for Riesman, autonomy accompanies all three.

Disorder in Order

These triads and others similar to them, when they have been reformulated as simultaneous presences rather than progressions, give us a glimpse of the infinitely complex subject with which sociology must come to grips. If we go a bit further certain heterodox propositions may be advanced. I would suggest the following: marginality is universal; everyone lives at the fringes of his society; all men are strangers. These sweeping and redundant generalizations most sociologists (including this one) would until recently have regarded as much too inclusive. Marginal men living at the fringes of society as strangers to one another were too conspicuous to deny, but they looked like exceptions. They now look like the rule. For this there are many reasons, most of them put in a nutshell by the sociologist Philip E. Slater: "Between any dynamic structure and its component parts there is potential conflict as well as substantial identity of goals. Otherwise, all structures would be tension-free and permanent, and exchange of components would never occur." [2]

We shall return through other labyrinthine paths to Slater's suggestive analysis. For the moment, let us pluck two phrases from this passage: "dynamic structure" and "exchange of components." Obviously the latter takes place in large part on account of the former. Very little exchange of components is imaginable without an antecedently dynamic culture. And it is dynamic because the exchange of components occurs without respite from birth to death. If no man is an island, neither is any family, tribe, moiety, clan, band, sect, class, club, sex, profession, generation, race, state, or nation. The dynamic structure churns and turns its members about, and they reciprocate in kind. After a social encounter has taken place, no one and nothing remain the same. The Great Wall of China could for a long time keep foreign bodies away from Cathay; it could not keep change from proceeding relentlessly behind those walls. There is something about a wall that human nature does not like, and a Marco Polo will

[2] "Social Bases of Personality," in *Sociology*, ed. Neil J. Smelser (New York: John Wiley and Sons, 1967), pp. 557–58.

sooner or later scale its heights. Failing that, one Chinese affects another who affects another and so on in a chain reaction leading to new customs and to an assault on the permeable wall, which finally collapses. Notice the phonological and morphological—let alone the semantic—change in any language, even that of a relatively isolated people, and you have a clue to what dynamic culture means on an intracultural level. Since a major source of social change is located in socialization, which makes for a certain refractoriness in every man, insularity from foreign influences cannot protect the "purity" of any culture.

Culture Contact

But there is no insularity. Through most of the eons in which "man made himself," he was a nomad. The agricultural revolution, the domestication of plants and animals, that great watershed, came late in human history. Until then the newly carnivorous species spent much of its energy roaming the reachable world in search of sustenance. We were a migratory race of fishermen, hunters, and food-gatherers. A stationary life was out of the question until men could settle down, harness other animals, irrigate the soil, and cultivate their own food. Even then, when herdsmen and husbandmen exhausted the land, they were compelled to forage for more, to move on in rhythmic peregrinations that took them far and near. The earth was not populous. Neither, with primitive tools, was much of it habitable. Scarcity prevailed, disease left its ravages, the physical danger to human survival was mysterious and perpetual. Small bands of kinsmen traveled from place to place, meeting and competing with one another. They traded, intermarried, and pooled resources or, more often, fought, slew, tortured, and subjugated rival bands. Prolonged association among close relatives hatched a myriad of little cultures, separate languages, unique patterns. Men were carriers of their cultures. They could not but collide with other men carrying different cultures. The ensuing interaction, friendly, neutral, or hostile, we call culture contact. Its technical name is acculturation, about which one must note a many-sidedness too frequently overlooked. Two or more cultures, through their human bearers, achieve contact, clash, meld, accommodate, regroup, and somehow come to terms. Neither one is ever the same again. Slaves are imported from Africa to the American South. They are acculturated in an alien plantation community, and so are their masters acculturated to them, quite as they once had been acculturated to people mistakenly named Indians. Even if every North American tribe had vanished, Indian cultures would still have left their mark on those who wiped them out. We must remember that culture is an *exchange* of components, implying a not necessarily equal but real and continuous mutuality.

The Persistence of the Simple in the Complex

We mingle from the first with others. Soon, many of the others are outsiders to us as we are outsiders to them. The "we group" or "in group," like the "primary group," the nuclear family, the play group of children, and the community of elders, is as salient a reality as ever. We unquestionably have deeper, more rounded, and more intimate relationships with those in our immediate social circle than with anyone else. By now, even in our world of large-scale organization and massive bureaucracy, "small-group" research has made this knowledge rather commonplace. In military combat, the protection of buddies (whether they belong to the Wehrmacht, to the Vietcong, or to the United States Army) matters more than high-flown war aims. Primary group morale on an assembly line will effect output more than directives from top or middle level management—and no less so under socialism than under capitalism. Data establishing the imperishability of "in" or "we" or "primary" groups could be piled higher than this little book. The more revealing point to be made about these groups in our present context is their ever-changing composition.

Primary groups, as they were first elucidated sixty years ago by Charles Horton Cooley, and as they continue to be known today, are small, intimate, face-to-face groups characterized by the sympathetic cooperation and continuous association of their members. Cooley indefensibly romanticized this type of group, and I have spilled my share of ink criticizing that tendency. Unfortunately, some of Cooley's successors are no wiser than their master. It is a controversy we need not rehearse. Indeed, even as a critic of Cooley, I am prepared to go further than he did: in light of the accumulated historical, sociological, psychological, and philosophical evidence, I would assert that the primary group is as indestructible as man. Primary groups have a way of crystallizing within every secondary group, every large corporate organization, every *Gesellschaft*. But those groups bubble, twist, shrink, expand, loosen, tighten, form, and re-form. It is as if they were in the grip of a cosmic kaleidoscope that fashions them into ever-different galaxies and constellations.

Why all this transience? The reasons are so many more than we have yet been able to apprehend that it behooves us to discuss only the most conspicuous of them. Among these, the incest taboo stands out as a cardinal, if not a decisive element. While the prohibition of incest is universal, its definition is not. At Yale University, George Peter Murdock developed, and his colleagues now preside over, the Human Relations Area Files where data on all known cultures, past and present, are classified into over eight hundred categories. If you skim through the material under "Incest," you will discover that it turns up everywhere, but in a profusion of inexplicable forms. And the forms are inconstant. They vary not only from place to place but from time to time in the same place. Our own state laws are a patchwork of inconsistency. Is marriage between first cousins incestuous? Not many years ago, after extended debate, the Michigan State Legislature decided that it was. Lovelorn Michiganders who happened to be first cousins and wished to marry sought the blessings of state and church in an adjoining jurisdiction where their wedding was legal.

The enormous variation in incest rules has never been satisfactorily explained. Most cultural anthropologists and family sociologists are content to report the variation. Some have been more venturesome in improvising theories to account for a universal law which, like all law and more than most, is ambiguously defined and fitfully enforced. The taboo sometimes extends only to parents and siblings, sometimes to "collateral" but not "parallel" cousins—depending on how blood ties are traced—often to larger and larger "family" units. Several hundred thousand members of the same clan in classical China were deemed to be so closely related that marriage between any two of them would somehow have been incestuous. At the opposite extreme, inbreeding reached a peak with brother-sister marriage (of which Cleopatra, for one, was by all accounts a fine flower) in Egyptian— and Incan—royal families. Exhaustive cross-cultural comparison turns up a few sparse and exotic cases in which father-daughter marriage is countenanced, but no case where mother-son marriage has been accepted.

When all is said and done, most of us most of the time have had to "marry out" and rather far out, at that. We moderns and post-moderns "marry in" along class, religious, ethnic, educational, and occupational lines (even "residential propinquity" makes it likely that a boy will marry the girl next door, if he or she stays put long enough to become nubile), but we too marry out along kinship lines.

For the sociologist, this is difficult and tricky terrain that we need not now attempt to traverse. The pertinent point to be made is that any and every incest taboo means exogamy ("marrying out"), and exogamy means not only movement from one primary group to another but from an in-group to an out-group. We either enter a family, clan, or tribe as strangers or accept others from outside, through marriage, into our midst. The human family begins with man. There is no prefamilial primate past, nor yet that "sexual communism," which an imaginative nineteenth-century theory conferred on "primitives." Given the universality of marriage, of legitimacy accorded only to offspring thereof, of an incest taboo and therefore of exogamy, the exchange of cultural components is ineluctable. Ferment resulting from the constant intrusion of external components keeps everybody somewhat out of phase, at least a bit off balance, consciously or unconsciously conveying some cultural items while tirelessly absorbing others.

The Interpenetration of Cultures

Marriage is migration; migration produces acculturation which results in new transactions that change every party to them. Clan exogamy is widespread in technologically underdeveloped parts of the world, say Oceania (including Polynesia, Melanesia, and Micronesia), Latin America, and Africa. In Africa alone we find more than nine hundred separate and distinct and therefore mutually unintelligible languages. Multiple marriage, especially among those in the upper strata of these societies, may be approved. It is entirely possible for a prestigious young man to marry into one or more alien language communities. His children are likely to be at least bilingual. It is not improbable that they will attend (or will until recently have attended) a Christian Mission school where Biblical and liturgical Latin are added to their linguistic baggage. Polyglot cultures require a lingua franca. Frequently, it is English, French, or Spanish which, when mixed with a local dialect, becomes pidgin English, pidgin French, or pidgin Spanish. An Indian in the tropical forests of Peru is better situated to be multilingual than a sophisticated resident of Lima. He lives in his Tower of Babel as we do in ours.

By invasion, out of economic necessity, simple greed, or inordinate acquisitiveness; from military and political adventurism; through cultural curiosity, the felt need for novelty, for lucrative opportunity, for religious liberty, to start afresh, to escape drudgery or shame at home; and not least, to be punished by exile for a common crime, to be impressed, captured, shanghaied, and sold into servitude and slavery: pick from this elliptical list, and you will know better why, although you were born at a particular dot on the globe, you foresook it for another dot where you will not long abide. Man is a species in motion; and a species in motion, however perilously it lives, cannot be a species in stagnation.

The Expanse of Civilizations

Man's origins seem to have been tropical. At first the species could best survive where nature was most bountiful. Ancient civilization, and not just the "Oriental Despotism" to which Karl Marx and Karl Wittfogel have referred, tends to be "hydraulic." Culture and nature intersect to form a watery womb for the birth of civilization. Agriculture is the midwife that delivers a civilizational entity on the cultivable banks of a river like the Nile, the Tigres, the Euphrates, the Yangtze. Ancient civilization grew and spread, germinating and decimating whole populations. Borrowing and lending, trading goods and ideas, overpowering neighbors in one way, only to be overpowered by them, every empire grew from the same transplanted seed that eventually destroyed it. Imperial soothsayers, philosophers, and statesmen, modern as well as ancient, sound a monotonous note. Over and over they deny the inroads made by culture contact, plumping for social and spiritual self-sufficiency. All of them express a hard half-truth rooted in reality; all display an institutional anxiety derived from simple ethnocentrism in small and relatively insular societies, which is greatly magnified by spokesmen for any far-flung imperium.

When George Washington, having helped lead his people out of the British Empire, declared his opposition to "foreign entanglements," he set the tone for American isolationism. President Washington could not have foreseen anything like an American Empire less than two centuries after his time, let alone a cry, a scrawl, a graffito in faraway places that invariably invited the American intruder to leave. Moreover, the slogan, "Yankee, go home!" is welcomed by a large percentage of Americans whose neoisolationism connects with a traditional isolationism older than the Republic. The intruder may be as unwilling as the host; each is animated by rage and resentment; neither can put a stop to what they fear above all—which is cultural contamination. And indeed the risk is real. Aliens demoralize and dispirit; they are a threat to unity and order; their presence is an anomaly. So, in their own tongues, spoke the prophets of Israel and the philosophers of Athens. All caught a glimpse of the truth. Those who echo them down through the ages ignore another and opposite but equally valid side of the truth: that aliens who demoralize and dispirit also energize and inspirit; that unity or order without leavening crumbles and molders; and that an anomaly is a challenge that can provoke creative responses. We are made human and we are latterly civilized by the same mercurial stuff that ultimately undoes us and all our works. As the will-to-live and the will-not-to-live (Freud's Eros and Thanatos) interminably struggle for supremacy, men continue to interact. They can scarcely choose not to do that. It is their glory and their misery.

And culture carriers interact. They do so through head-on collisions or tangential contact, but in any case as bearers of a mixture that acts upon while it is being acted upon by bearers of another mixture. If today fewer overarching cultures exist because of a vast improvement in transportation and communication, then more subcultures proliferate within each culture. Exactly the same kind of pressure that homogenizes a previously very heterogeneous world population, say industrialism, also serves to diversify its members. Our neighbors are nearer and more numerous as supersonic flight and television pictures bouncing off a stellar satellite bring them within hailing distance. At the same time, they are sociologically further away and more estranged from one another than ever before. Even without pernicious "survivals," customs that have outlived their utility, it would be difficult to achieve transcultural peace and understanding. With machine production soaring to automation in a computerized economy, men are brought together, and with it, as increasing specialization fosters a steadily greater division of labor, they are once again torn apart.

The "Borrowing of Culture"

To be near and yet to be far: is this not the *condition humaine*? Goethe speaks not just for himself, but for the meanest and least perceptive of us when he cries, "Nothing human is alien to me." We do have empathy for others. Any human act, however distant and repugnant, can be more or less understood. This indeed is the bedrock of *Verstehen* sociology. It prostulates that we are capable of *motivational* as well as *observational* understanding. These are cumbersome translations of Max Weber's terminology. They awkwardly indicate the major difference between natural or physical and social science. The natural scientist working in physics or chemistry or biology can understand, always provisionally, how something happens. He is forever barred from understanding *why* it happens. To ask why something happens in the natural universe is to raise a theological or metaphysical question that does not fall within one's purview as a scientist. Each of the physical sciences has developed superb methods, some better than others, by which to test, verify or falsify, revise, and perfect hypotheses. Some of these methods, notably those related to observation rather than experimentation, are useful to some social scientists. They have the great advantage of providing objectivity, a goal toward which every scientist must strive. The subject matter of physical science is such that its practitioners need not worry about those personal prejudices that plague social science. Dilthey and Weber admit this difference. Yet they are champions of social science. For their subject matter, which is meaningful (and therefore human) interaction, not only allows but demands the question, "Why?" And that question, with the aid of *Einfühlung*, empathy, insight, rapport, or whatever else one cares to call this quality, is always answerable up to a point. It is answerable up to that point because—to use an old-fashioned phrase—"the psychic unity of mankind" makes us sociologically at one with others who despite their biological and cultural diversity, are a single interbreeding species.

Since every discovery introduces new mysteries, we shall almost certainly never understand anything in this world fully and finally. And we shall probably continue to understand less about man-in-society than about nature-at-large. In our daily lives, in our random contacts, even in our intimate associations, we get on with others by sharing their imputations, their definitions, their interpretations, and their delusions. The closer we are to one or more vis-à-vis, the greater our sharing; and our sharing of symbols, images, and gestures enlarges the understanding between us. Since human beings, divided and subdivided as they are, can recognize situations common to them all, they are in some measure attuned to every other member of their species. In no matter how attenuated a manner, the surviving creature of a Stone Age culture responds to a European sophisticate—and vice versa—with more understanding than either can ever have for non-human beings. It is this kind of closeness that sociology attempts to systematize. The closeness is communicable. Art, without doubt, demonstrates it better than science, but no science is so without art as to be devoid of essential metaphors, and sociology is as much art as science. It treats of man, a unique blend of emotion and cognition, of outwardness and inwardness.

One human being, often dubbed "Ego" in sociological analysis, observes an act undertaken by "Alter," another human being. Ego's act, whatever it may be, is potentially comprehensible to any number of Alters. They can always learn why he does what he does: builds a fire, beats a drum, paints a wall, sings a chant, and so on ad infinitum. And Ego knows why he is doing what he is doing. We "understand" relatives, friends, and neighbors more or less effortlessly. Their motivations are as clear to us as our own. One reflects the other. With greater strain and more imagination, we achieve minimal rapport with people who come from afar. If Ego grossly misunderstands and reacts inappropriately, his error can be explained to him. So, through the comprehensible meaning of their external acts, do men preserve their psychic or inner or intersubjective unity.

Cultural "Misunderstanding" and Creativity

As Anselm Strauss suggests in the title to his stimulating book about human society, it is an amalgam of *Mirrors and Masks*.[3] But the mirrors distort and the masks deceive. The Looking-Glass Self comes back to us through a cracked mirror of symbolic representations. Man walks all his days through a fun house whose principal corridor is a hall of mirrors in which one possibly extended, or distended, swollen or shrunken, but surely cock-eyed apparition follows another. Our social life is a series of such standardized misperceptions. If we do largely see ourselves as others see us, then it is through many a glass and ever so darkly.

But man does not live by mirrors alone. He adds masks, donning and discarding them as the occasion arises. This permits him to dissociate action from attitude. By dissembling, by simulating, by deliberately misleading and deceiving, he can hide and hug his true or private self. Volition comes into play. When a society is beset with political upheaval, the conservative who inwardly opposes change may choose to fly his true colors (and few do) or act canny and cautious, pretending to be the revolutionary he inwardly despises (and the many can be counted on to do that). They exert their will

[3] Anselm Strauss, *Mirrors and Masks* (New York: Free Press, 1954).

by behaving "inauthentically" and thereby run the risk of expending and exhausting it. Veils that were intended merely to hide the truth from others then end up by concealing it from their wearers as well. Of guises and disguises there is no limit, nor therefore of deceptions and self-deceptions. So, although superficial understanding of overt acts makes social relations (and sociology) possible, deep, real, thorough understanding is forever beyond us. We can never fully understand another, and not simply because we are not the other, have not lived his life or experienced the unrepeatable events that impinged upon him, but, worse luck, for precisely the same reasons that we can never fully understand ourselves.

The sociologist does not lay down his tools before this mystery, which it would nonetheless be derelict of him not to acknowledge. He goes on debunking, unmasking, lifting veils, and dispelling illusions. Only so will he enlarge his understanding of phenomena that ultimately baffle him, and baffle him the more he learns about them. The physicist is in a similar predicament—with the difference that his findings do not directly alter the cosmos he studies, whereas greater understanding of self and others is itself a change-agent at work on both. If I understand myself and yourself better than before, then we stand in a different relationship to each other; and new mysteries unfold that require further sociological exploration. It is often said that Karl Marx came to grief by failing to calculate the weight of his own thought upon future generations. The impeachment is a just one. Sociologists would do well to avoid his error by taking systematically into account the effect of their understanding, not least through its creation of further widely dispersed misunderstanding.

Men will go on understanding each other up to a point, and they will go on misunderstanding each other beyond that point. Up to that point, no man is an island, and beyond that point every man is an island. No sociological explanation is worth much unless it incorporates this circumstance: that we are no less out of touch with our fellows and ourselves than we are in touch with them. Men communicate among themselves just as George Herbert Mead said they do. One of us makes a gesture, usually verbal; the other interprets that gesture—and whether he does so without delay or after prolonged consideration does not matter—and then, on that basis, he responds; and his gesture is in turn interpreted, but how fast or how accurately will depend upon countless variables. Symbols, above all words, give the *genus humanum* his humanity. It is a long time since Francis Bacon wrote about the "Imperfection of Words," but little has been done and little more can be done to overcome that imperfection. Your vocabulary and mine overlap, and so we reach each other after a fashion. Where our words are not the same, although both of us may be expressing ourselves only in English, we are still not speaking the same language. My professional jargon—a so-called "special" language of the type peculiar to those engaged in a particular occupation or those who pursue a common interest—can only be jabberwocky to the uninitiated. Whoever uses a special language (and who does not?) belongs to a confraternity—it is not too much to say a community or a communion—out of which his idiom has sprung. Despite the shared understandings that unify us and exclude outsiders, I would be foolhardy to assume that my colleagues appreciate all the overtones and undertones of a message I have concocted for nobody else but them. Mathematicians do not fret about this problem. They have designed an esoteric system of notations that admirably suits their purposes. The most elegant of these is symbolic logic, a fine product of the human mind, a game (and not to be taken lightly as such: game theory is heady stuff), an artificial language whose precision and exactitude no natural language can approach. In the empirical world of day-to-day affairs, we have no substitute for natural language with all its inherent fuzziness, vagueness, imprecision, and inexactitude.

Indigenous Change

The natural language of a people is serviceable enough. It preserves sounds, signs, and meanings and transforms them all. Like every other facet of culture, it is fixed in flux, a splendid example of the popular saying, that, "Change is immutable." Language, with its unlimited absorptive capacity, is as impermanent and as structured as man himself. Its resiliency and order are matched by his. An individual who remains in the community of his birth never stops learning at least one vital, changeable, flexible, beautifully clear, and hope-lessly ambiguous language. Let him depart for long, without having totally lost his mother tongue, and he will come home like Odysseus returning to Ithaca, lost in a mist of unfamiliarity. For him every-thing is the same, and nothing is the same. The surroundings are similar but different; so are the words. He will have forgotten some; others were coined in his absence. His is the exacerbated case of a universal confusion. Odysseus must speak in many tongues, and not seldom, with a forked tongue as well. At last, while more comfortable in his mother tongue, he is still not at home with it. Odysseus is Everyman. Homer speaks to us over the ages partly because, like his hero, each of us wanders—and wonders why he can never be fully understood either by his fellowman or by himself.

Man is a wanderer by nature, and not much less so if he stays put than if he moves about. In either case his craving for new experience in time and over space will be met. W. I. Thomas, in a famous formu-lation, singled out that craving as the first of four wishes basic to man. Thomas wrote in 1924:

> The desire for new experience is seen in simple form in the prowling and meddling activities of the child, and the love of adventure and travel in the boy and man. It ranges in moral quality from the pursuit of game and the pursuit of pleasure to the pursuit of knowledge and the pursuit of ideals. It is found equally in the vagabond and in the scientific explorer. Novels, theaters, motion pictures, etc., are means of satisfying the desire vicariously, and their popularity is a sign of the elemental force of this desire.
>
> In its pure form the desire for new experience implies motion, change, danger, instability, social irresponsibility. The individual dom-inated by it shows a tendency to disregard prevailing standards and group interests. He may be a complete failure, on account of his in-stability; or a conspicuous success, if he converts his experiences into social values—puts them in the form of a poem, makes of them a contribution to science, etc.[4]

And yet this powerful, positive, and elemental wish is promptly undercut by another, the desire for security, about which Thomas writes that it "is opposed to the desire for new experience." Further:

---

[4] W. I. Thomas, "The Person and His Wishes, in *Introduction to the Science of Sociology*, eds. Robert E. Park and Ernest W. Burgess (Chicago: University of Chicago Press, 1924), p. 488.

"It implies avoidance of danger and death, caution, conservatism. Incorporation in an organization (family, community, state) provides the greatest security." [5] The tension between these two wishes is heightened by two other wishes, which are the desire for recognition and the desire for response. Since these wishes or prime movers relate to radically different public and private spheres, they too are at loggerheads. To satisfy one is to frustrate the other. The desire for recognition is expressed in a broad array of devices all aimed at securing public distinction. Consequently:

> A list of the different modes of seeking recognition would be very long. It would include courageous behavior, the showing off of our ornament and dress, the pomp of kings, the display of opinions and knowledge, the possession of special attainments—in the arts, for example. It is expressed in arrogance and in humility, even in martyrdom. Certain modes of seeking recognition we define as "ambition." The "will to power" belongs here. Perhaps there has been no spur to activity so keen and no motive so naively avowed as the desire for "undying fame," and it would be difficult to estimate the role the desire for recognition has played in the creation of social values. [6]

Notwithstanding the keenness and inestimably important role of this fundamental wish, it is contradictory to the fourth and final wish. Thomas caps his theory of motivation with "the desire for response" which is a craving for "the more intimate appreciation of individuals." As such it is opposed to man's equally strong desire for recognition from the public at large. The desire for personal response is "exemplified in mother-love (touch plays an important role in this connection), in romantic love, family affection, and other personal attachments." [7]

For Thomas, this catalogue comprehends all "the positive" wishes. Only when any or all of them are thwarted are we troubled by the appearance of negative attitudes like anger, fear, hate, and prejudice. Indeed, "Our hopes, fears, inspirations, joys, sorrows, are bound up with these wishes and issue from them." [8] Thomas implicitly concedes the irreconcilability of his wishes and the inevitability of their frus-

[5] Loc. cit.
[6] Ibid., p. 489.
[7] Loc. cit.
[8] Ibid., p. 490.

tration. If, as he admits, a single act may contain a plurality of wishes and one negates another, then "negative attitudes" are statistically normal. How could it be otherwise when Thomas posits "a kaleidoscopic mingling of wishes throughout life"? Their hypothetical convergence only serves to accentuate the difficulty of putting it all together:

> Thus when a peasant emigrates to America he may expect to have a good time and learn many things (new experiences), to make a fortune (greater security), to have a higher social standing on his return (recognition), and to induce a certain person to marry him (response).[9]

Migration and Social Change

Peasants emigrating to urban America were a matter of special concern to Thomas and his great collaborator, Florian Znaniecki. Their monumental study of the Polish peasant in America offers human documents, personal correspondence, and public papers, all filled with disappointment, disenchantment, and disorganization. Thomas and Znaniecki wrote at the flood tide of mass migration to these shores. During those years before restrictive legislation reduced that tide to a trickle, an average of a million or more immigrants per annum reached the United States. Early in this century, more than half the total population of our largest cities was composed of foreign-born persons. They painfully accommodated to the shifting scene before them, as Thomas, Znaniecki, and the whole "Chicago school" of American sociology, led at that time by Robert Park, duly noted. That they also *contributed,* unevenly but heavily, by acculturative interaction, through kaleidoscopic mingling, is a fact that the Chicago school surprisingly slighted. We can no longer overlook the *give* in a give-and-take relationship.

Polish Americans, like Irish Americans and Italian Americans, German and Dutch Americans, Eastern European Jews, Hungarian, Ukrainian, and Russian Americans: did they not transform the urban landscape as much as they were transformed by it? Second and third

[9] Loc. cit.

generation Americans from Europe and Asia encounter the grand-
children of black slaves. An indigenous people whose ancestors probably crossed the Bering Straits long before Christopher Columbus
or Leif Ericson arrived in this hemisphere, refuses to accept cultural
extinction. Early settlers' descendants crisscross at the intersections
of ever-widening social circles. An infusion of Latin Americans, of
Mexicans, Puerto Ricans, and Panamanians changes the social climate.
They bring a multitude of their customs and shed some, while diffus-
ing and absorbing others. Into this flux, as into Heraclitus's river, we
"step and do not step." Similarly, as Heraclitus was the first to suggest, we can never step twice into the same flux or the same river.
It is for this reason that men in their eternal flux are simultaneously
far and near. Strangers to one another and to themselves, their agreements precede disagreements that lead to further agreements. Heraclitus, the pre-Socratic genius of Ephesus, taught this sociological
paradox too, as we learn from one of his most valuable fragments:
"To be in agreement is to differ; the concordant is the discordant.
From out of all the many particulars comes oneness, and out of oneness come all the particulars." [10] With this proposition our ideologues
have constructed the theory of American exceptionalism. American
universalism would be closer to the philosophical and sociological
truth. Mass migration has thrust ethnically and culturally diverse
human beings together on every continent where they have always
striven with and against one another. The American Dream, a gentler
name for the American delusion, in its essence consists of two mis-
conceptions. The first misconception is merely parochial, assuming
that a vast racial, ethnic, and sociocultural conglomeration over one
territorial expanse is very special. In fact, anywhere on earth and at
any point in time, only its absence is special. To look about us at
this moment without so much as scratching a narrow surface that
would reveal much more, we see, ad libitum: Jews and Arabs, Flem-
ings and Walloons, Greeks and Turks, Hindus and Moslems, French
and English Canadians. How they and their counterparts struggle to
coexist or to gain the upperhand and subdue their countrymen! The
second misconception is precisely that here alone in America such

[10] Heraclitus, "Fragments," in *The Presocratics*, ed. Philip Wheelwright (New
York: Odyssey, 1966), p. 48.

differences would disappear. They were to have gone up in a common vapor of harmony and homogeneity produced by the great American melting pot. A double and triple melting pot has not succeeded where the single melting pot so signally failed. It is of small consequence whether one's own group happens to be on a front or a back burner. The group softens under great heat only to harden once again. The pot is also a forge. So America takes on a certain shapelessness even while it is all of a piece. The same must be said of Britain, with embattled Orangemen in Northern Ireland and Welshmen outdoing Scots in their bid for "devolution" or local autonomy; for the USSR, where the so-called minorities outnumber the official majority of Great Russians; for India, a subcontinent heaving with swarms of antipathetic peoples; and for most of the new nations of Africa arbitrarily united along frontiers drawn by those who colonized and left many a trace but papered over an intertribal animosity that can only go on erupting in strife and warfare.

Urbanization

In most of the world, urbanization as a prerequisite to modernization is just gathering steam. A recent West African monograph is appropriately entitled *Strangers to the City: Urban Man in Jos, Nigeria,* and although the author only deals with one city, he does so because of its representativeness. Not that pre-industrial cities are new in Africa. They have not only existed for centuries, but, "Many African people had direct or indirect commercial, political and cultural transactions with Europeans and Asians (including Chinese and Indonesians) since before the time of Christ. . . ." World War II abruptly cast most of Africa into the modern commercial world. By the end of that war, it was no longer possible to find "an African tribesman untouched by European influences." [11] Young Africans fought alongside Allied soldiers in Ethiopia, Burma, India, and Europe; and Western military contingents were stationed in many parts of black Africa. More significantly:

[11] Leonard Plotnicov, *Strangers to the City: Urban Man in Jos, Nigeria* (Pittsburgh: University of Pittsburgh Press, 1967), p. 5.

The production of peasant cash crops, plantation crops, and sylvan and mineral raw materials was initiated or vastly increased to meet emergency demands. Large numbers of men were mobilized to provide the labor for these efforts and, concurrently, cities mushroomed from small settlements. Military bases were located in towns and, to speed international communications, deep-water harbors and airports were constructed. . . . Wage work and industrial entrepreneurship became the accepted pattern of adult economic life, and men moved to and fro between areas of employment and their homes. Many responded to economic opportunities by living either for long periods or permanently in urban centers. In short, the industrial revolution had at last come to Africa.[12]

What does this mean in human terms for Jos, the north Nigerian new city under study, and for its sixty thousand inhabitants? For most residents,

The cultural milieu of Jos is different from their traditional way of life. . . . The people feel alien to that city in two ways: geographically and culturally. By their own admission they say that they reside in a foreign land and that "home" is elsewhere, often several hundred miles distant. Even the tribal peoples native to the area around Jos, who are honorifically referred to as the "owners of the land," regard their Jos residences in the same way and look upon native villages in the vicinity as their true homes.[13]

Emerging African cities are composed of people drawn from diverse tribal societies mixed with Levantines, Indians, and Europeans; religious affiliations vary from Christian and Muslim sects to traditional African cults. Role consistency, never very marked anywhere, is even less discernible in this cultural hodgepodge. "For example, a well-educated African who might be acknowledged as a pillar of his local Christian congregation, might also have several wives, worship his ancestral spirits, employ traditional medicines and talismans for himself and his family, and successfully run a transport business using modern organizational methods."[14] A case can be made for African exceptionalism. It would be exactly as strong and as misleading as

[12] Ibid., p. 6.
[13] Ibid., pp. 3–4.
[14] Ibid., p. 7.

the case for American exceptionalism. Urban Africa does present unique cultural and organizational expressions. But, to those who have taken a hard look at the phenomenon, "It has also become more apparent that similar underlying conditions in modern, cosmopolitan centers, composed of heterogeneous and/or stratified populations, occur all over the world." [15] Urban life itself, we are now being told, "presents problems of a similar character and calls for organizations of much the same kind to deal with these problems." The sociologist can only add, "but of course—for city people, like country people, are as alike as they are unalike." Ceaseless motion alone makes for a finite number of similarities and an infinite number of contrasts. Even the catatonic patient in a mental hospital whose limbs are paralyzed moves intrapsychically, whether or not he and his attendants realize it. And cultural catatonia, with its generalized paralysis and absolute petrifaction, cannot be a social problem.

Multiform man is always on the go from one way station to another. He wriggles, jumps, dances, rides, and flies, a body never at rest, seeking or avoiding other such bodies, but willy-nilly, colliding with them. Inherently ambivalent, filled with love and hate, with sympathy and antipathy, endowed with a triadic nature that makes him all at once religious, metaphysical, and positivistic—or something approximately equivalent to that—motivated by at least four fundamentally constructive wishes, each subject to frustration and conversion into its opposite, he soon moves out into a kaleidoscopic world and swells to multivalent proportions. Philip Slater's "substantial identity of goals" cannot persist. "Potential conflict" is remorselessly translated into real conflict between "any dynamic structure"—for there is no other kind—and its component parts.

Robert Jay Lifton sees something oddly protean about youth in certain parts of Asia, and associates the trait with a new kind of modern man.[16] Two existentialist sociologists, Stanford M. Lyman and Marvin B. Scott, believe that Shakespeare had his arch villain, Richard III, place "the persona ahead of the self, the performance ahead of the reality, and in doing so captured the general qualities

---

[15] Ibid., p. 5.

[16] Robert Jay Lifton, "Protean Man," in *History and Human Survival*, ed. John Simon (New York: Random House, 1970), pp. 311–31.

of *Machiavelli's* and *modern society's* man." [17] (My italics.) Through Richard's lips Shakespeare says:

> Why I can smile, and murder while I smile,
> And cry "Content" to that which grieves my heart
> And wet my cheeks with artificial tears,
> And frame my face to all occasions. . . .
> I'll play the orator as well as Nestor,
> Deceive more slyly than Ulysses could,
> And, like a Sinon, take another Troy.
> I can add colours to the chameleon,
> Change shapes with Proteus for advantages,
> And set the murderous Machiavelli to school.

Shakespeare, as usual, captured more than the general qualities of a specific time, his or ours. The greatest of poets knew that man is never more himself than when he is Proteus.

The necessary imagery is nearly complete when we add that man, no matter what his Adamic nature, is also and above all, Cain. Jacques Ellul, a profound sociologist and a committed theologian, strikes just the right note on this theme. Let us round off this chapter by taking a leaf out of his book:

> The first builder of a city was Cain. The circumstances were these:
> After he had murdered his brother, Cain was summoned by God and cursed: "When you till the ground, it shall no longer yield to you its strength; you shall be a fugitive and a wanderer on the earth."
> But Cain is afraid that he himself will surely be killed in revenge: "My punishment is greater than I can bear. Behold thou has driven me this day from the ground; and from thy face I shall be hidden; and I shall be a fugitive and a wanderer on the earth."
> The Lord, however, says to him, "If anyone slays Cain vengeance shall be taken upon him sevenfold." So "the Lord put a mark on Cain, lest anyone who came upon him should kill him."
> And "then Cain went away from the presence of the Lord, and dwelt in the Land of Nod, east of Eden." And he "knew his wife, and she conceived and bore Enoch; and he built a city, and called the name of the city after the name of his son Enoch." [18]

---

[17] Stanford M. Lyman and Marvin B. Scott, *A Sociology of the Absurd* (New York: Appleton-Century-Crofts, 1970), p. 20.

[18] Jacques Ellul, *The Meaning of the City* (Grand Rapids, Mich.: W. B. Eerdmans Publishing Company, 1970), p. 1.

To Ellul, the historicity of this fable is of little importance. He laughs at the geographers who say they have been unable to locate a historical land of Nod: "Unknown to geographers. And what kind of land would it be, this Nowhere land, which is not a place but a lack of place, the opposite of Eden, another country unknown to geographers?" [19]

We all inhabit the land of *Nod*, a Hebrew word whose literal translation is the land of wandering. There man as Cain comes and goes "in his futile search for eternity," seeking security, struggling against external marauders, and the demons within, unable to retrace his steps, permanently deprived of God's protection. He and we are forever vagabonds, fugitives, strangers, one and all condemned to life, to freedom, and to change.

For Further Consideration

1. What are the various forms of social change?
   Describe each briefly.
2. How is exogamy related to social change?
3. Does the American melting pot produce a common culture? Why? Why not?

[19] Loc. cit.

THIS has been a brief exploratory trip. We have had time only for glimpses of a vast expanse to which, one hopes, the traveler will return for further study. Herman Melville, after completing his masterpiece, *Moby Dick,* could cry: "This whole book is but a draft—nay, but a draft of a draft. Oh, Time, Strength, Cash, and Patience!" Melville, sailor, whaler, stranger, and homebody, America's sovereign romancer: did he not circumnavigate the inner and outer world we all inhabit? Whoever has not read him or his peers and betters is wasting time with the likes of us. And yet was he not right that even *Moby Dick* is no more than the draft of a draft? Lesser lights who claim more should be laughed out of court. Still, if their work deserves the slightest attention, it will end without ever having been finished.

A Personal Testament

We began by asking the virtually unanswerable question: What is sociology? During most of my lifetime—and I shall soon have been

Epilogue

around half a century—the word "sociology" seemed to be gathering more and more coherence. The new clarity moved in a direction that so displeased me and friends of mine who practiced "my kind" of sociology that we thought to stop calling ourselves sociologists. Positivism in the social sciences coupled with something the late C. Wright Mills rightly put down as "abstracted theory" did not appeal to us. We regarded ourselves as a tiny band fighting for sociology with a human face, and the battle looked hopeless. As punch cards replaced people, many of us began to feel what others said about our "value-free" discipline, that it was also valueless.

"We happy few" learned most of our sociology from European scholars who barely escaped Hitler's clutches; they were rescued and repaid us several times over in the precious coin of cosmopolitan humanism. Each one of these men personified the "detached concern" that ought always to have been the nucleus of our personal and professional ethic. Social scientists like Hans Gerth, Albert Salomon, Ernst Kris, Hans Speier, Emil Lederer, Alfred Schütz, Carl Mayer, and, for awhile, such hyphenated sociologists as Georges Gurvitch, Claude Lévi-Strauss, and T. W. Adorno enormously enriched all that they touched. Not wholly disdaining the empiricism of American sociology, these learned men taught us to temper it, tame and limit it, broaden and widen it. For students who heeded them in my generation the effect they had may, in a modest way, be likened to that of refugee artists sparking and invigorating their hesitant American counterparts during the Second World War. We learned from the example they set to judge ourselves by a set of standards so high that no one could fully meet them. Who would ever match these peerless scholars? We prized our teachers all the more as it became obvious that they were irreplaceable. A special milieu produced them—and it was wiped out. Our hope can only be to keep their spirit alive. In the world of ideas, they judged others and themselves with some severity, and it would be a betrayal of their legacy for us to do less. They were creative intellectuals who synthesized European and American theory, wedded pragmatism and phenomenology, combined Kant with James or Jefferson, exposed the Saint Simonian roots of Veblenian ideology, instructed us in how to read texts with a philologist's care, all the while stimulating students' critical faculties until fledglings were shaken out of their sluggish parochialism.

The marriage of Weimar and American culture left us with a rich dowry which it would be a tragedy to dissipate. Not that the European savants were faultless. Some were fakers or pedants or opportunists; others, among whom some have been the longest-lived, were all three. But without the best of them, none of us would be nearly so well equipped to tell phony goods from the real thing.

The Sociologist, Evanescence, and Constancy

The best of them also illustrate a major theme of this outline for the draft of a draft of a book. Their unsettled, migratory, uprooted, and restless lives brought to exquisite ripeness much that I have randomly tried to articulate from sources that might not have occurred to me without their inspiration. Movement, friction, change, conflict, paradox, flux, choice, freedom, decay, death, and renewal, all inside a Chinese box covered with constraint and continuity: one could not contemplate who our teachers were or what they thought and fail to be obsessed with these concepts which, however, did not belong to the mainstream of our profession. If they ever do, it will be necessary to criticize them with the same vigor we apply to all generally accepted concepts, principles, conventions, and fashions. It nevertheless appears in the present state of scientific knowledge and philosophical reflection that our mentors did impart a glimmering of wisdom to us.

Without it, how could we begin to grasp a world so torn and convulsed, so divided and subdivided, so close to possible extinction that anthropologists have begun to speak of themselves as entropologists? Maybe the sociological unit of study, man himself, is running down and out. If so, will that be the end? Or just another transformation, a social and genetic mutation? Our overloaded planet may be subject to the second law of thermodynamics, but astronomers say that man lives in an expanding universe, with stars and galaxies racing away from each other like bits of debris from a single explosion. This phenomenon might be part of a cosmic cycle in which all matter alternately explodes from a central mass, and then regroups to explode again. If heavenly bodies display such rhythmic activity, so do tiny atoms and any one-celled amoeba in its streaming protoplasm, which is the stuff of life. With these scientific vistas before us, the already obsolete stress on social statics has to look like even more of an aberration than we originally suspected. Fixated on social statics, sociology could not cope with living men and organic societies. It was unprepared for change in them or in itself. Both changed. How right Mills was in the fifties when he wanted to call his critique of the dominant functionalism, methodologism, and scientism an autopsy. Hans Gerth, probably more than anyone else, had alerted him to the evanescence of everything that nevertheless remains partially constant.

Now the institutional movement toward deauthorization and delegitimation has an incidental parallel in sociology. We already hear talk of a growth crisis, for Auguste Comte's unpedigreed brainchild has flourished and spread. The field established by unattached intellectuals has moved into academic, governmental, commercial, and theological institutions. "Yet," writes Edward Tiryakian, "in the face of newly found public prestige and widening acceptance, sociology is developing internal disruptions of increasing severity . . . and the fissures are becoming very plain to behold at annual meetings of the sociological profession." [1] In a satirical dictionary (compiled a year or so ago when such lexicography looked more attractive than the sociology that was too much with me) I playfully defined sociology as: "An academic discipline in which radical activists, realizing that its scientific pretensions are laughable and its political implications reprehensible, enroll in unprecedented numbers." Sociology booms and busts. Thus a clever sociologist of sociology like Tiryakian deduces a growth crisis, "or more aptly put" (we would say, "more fashionably put"), "an identity crisis." What does the crisis mean? Tiryakian is on solid ground when he replies, "It means basically that sociology is part and parcel of the existential whole of society . . . its manifestations in different countries are not accidental but rather part of the sociohistorical becoming of the larger social world to which sociology is linked by various ties." [2]

These phrases, "the existential whole of society" and "sociohistorical becoming," go far toward explaining what sociology and its subject

[1] Edward A. Tiryakian, *The Phenomenon of Sociology: A Reader in the Sociology of Sociology* (New York: Appleton-Century-Crofts), p. 1.
[2] Ibid., p. 2.

matter really are. I think that in the past no one understood this better than Weber, Simmel, Marx, and Durkheim. We can still profit from going to school to them, not as worshipful disciples but as appreciative students. If from their social heritage we fastidiously pick and choose, our action will cast us into the "existential whole of society." There we need to be neither rudderless nor bound in dry-dock. Properly equipped, the apprentice scholar will experience socio-cultural becoming even as he observes and analyzes it in his own or anyone else's society. Some years ago, Leo W. Simmons recorded and edited an autobiography of Don Talayesva, a Hopi Indian. Don was a direct descendant of people who have lived in this hemisphere for over two thousand years. While preserving certain contours of their own distinctive culture, they have had their share of dissension, warfare, acculturation, innovation, migration, deviation, destruction, and restoration. Any anthropological account of Hopi history will suffice to dispel old myths about "primitive" stagnation. In a recent foreword to Simmons's superb monograph, Robert V. Hine points out that for the anthropologist as amanuensis, it is important to note in each situation whether Don was "a creature, a carrier, or a manipulator of the mores." [3] My point throughout this book is precisely that man always survives by being creature, carrier, *and* manipulator of the mores. It is necessary to note all three in the life history of a specific individual, group, society, or culture.

No one among our contemporaries does this with better skill than Sir Geoffrey Vickers, the urbane English polymath. By looking back and stopping to ponder what has happened to us, Sir Geoffrey sees further than most futurologists. He spotted a fundamental error in Comte's formula (to know in order to predict and to predict in order to control) for the physical sciences no less than for the social sciences. What has happened is rather that

> during the past two centuries, men gained knowledge, which vastly increased their ability to predict and control; and they used these powers to make a world increasingly unpredictable and uncontrollable. This paradoxical result flowed from the fact that the technologies to

[3] Robert V. Hine, "Foreword" in *Sun Chief*, ed. Leo W. Simmons (New Haven: Yale University Press, 1970), p. xii.

which science gave birth enabled man not only to predict but also to alter the course of events in his milieu.[4]

It should be clear from our ecological fix that man has not subdued nature and from our social fix that he is not about to subdue human nature. His primordial power to alter the environment, tremendously enhanced by modern science, never brought increased control over it. Instead we are at present in what Sir Geoffrey describes as the last stage of a free fall: a fall from the agricultural into the industrial epoch; from a natural into a man-made world; and so "into an increasingly political world, a world so unpredictable that it demands to be regulated." How? Through the use of institutions that do not yet exist.

I especially admire the wonder with which Geoffrey Vickers, this accomplished Englishman, summarizes what should be sociological commonplaces, and therefore take the liberty of quoting him in extenso:

> It is a fact strange beyond comprehension that the whole corpus of human knowledge is relearned at least three times each century; and this becomes even stranger when we remember that what is relearned is not only the technological skills and knowledge which serve our common needs, but also the political and cultural ways of thinking and feeling and acting which determine what we shall conceive our common needs to be, and how we shall pursue them. Every one of us not long ago lay in cradle, helpless and speechless, unable to distinguish one thing from another, even self from no-self, equipped with only a few reflexes, a unique genetic code, and a learning potential. Whatever we are now, our readiness to notice this and ignore that, to accept this as a commitment while we dismiss that as having no claim on us, to enjoy or accept relations of one sort and to hate or resent others—all this we have learned from our experience of the culture into which we were born; and it is increasingly this which determines how we shall accept and interpret new experience. This is the process by which each new generation is incorporated into and inherits the society into which it is born, and through which alone it is socialized and humanized.[5]

There we have in a nutshell what whole textbooks tell us. And then we have what needs to be added:

[4] Sir Geoffrey Vickers, *Value Systems and Social Process* (Harmondsworth, England: Penguin Books, 1970), p. 49.
[5] Ibid., pp. 77–78.

Yet how far from passive is the acceptance of heritage! How selective are these learners, how much they amplify, change or reject! For at least a dozen generations now, each generation has had more to transmit, to add, and to change than the generation before.[6]

The acceleration of change is real enough, but so is its constancy, and my only warning would be that we do not allow myopia to keep us from seeing the latter for the former.

Credo

Rapid change spells disintegration. We live in the midst of environmental rot. Many men despair as they circle the ruins around them. Geoffrey Vickers is no Pollyanna; neither does he succumb to an end-of-the-world psychology. Once again, a short statement of his beautifully condenses what this book is all about:

> When the first seed-bearing plants began to release their seeds to the wind's distribution, no mind could have foretold, if mind had been there to speculate, that rooting and dying on the infertile wastes, their own decay would build up a bed of humus in which unimagined successors would evolve and flourish. We are guardians of a social humus more precious and more vulnerable than theirs—guardians not merely of values but of the soil in which values grow. That seedbed is today menaced by a vastly increased erosion. Conservators and innovators alike, our paramount duty to the future is to leave it a little deeper for our passage.[7]

I do not know a better credo than this one. Students, colleagues, fellow men and women, let us cultivate our own sense of humus.

[6] Ibid., p. 78.
[7] Ibid., pp. 84–85.

Index